Sweet & Simple
Country Cross-Stitch

Lori Gardner

Sweet & Simple
Country Cross-Stitch

Lori Gardner

Sterling Publishing Co., Inc. New York
A Sterling/Chapelle Book

Chapelle Ltd.

Owner:
Jo Packham

Editor:
Leslie Ridenour

Staff:
Marie Barber, Malissa Boatwright, Kass Burchett,
Rebecca Christensen, Holly Fuller, Marilyn Goff, Amber Hansen,
Michael Hannah, Shirley Heslop, Holly Hollingsworth,
Susan Jorgensen, Pauline Locke, Barbara Milburn, Linda Orton,
Pat Pearson, Karmen Quinney, and Cindy Stoeckl

Photography:
Kevin Dilley, photographer for Hazen Photography

Photo Stylists:
Lori Gardner, Susan Laws, Jo Packham, and Cindy Rooks

All frames were designed, painted, and finished by Lori Gardner
and her assistant, Lisa Atwood.

Library of Congress Cataloging-in-Publication Data

Gardner, Lori.
    Sweet & simple country cross-stitch / Lori Gardner.
        p.   cm.
    "A Sterling/Chapelle book."
    Includes index.
    ISBN 0-8069-9341-3
    1. Cross-stitch—Patterns. 2. Decoration and ornament, Rustic.
I. Title.
TT778.C76G38 1997
746.46'041--dc21   96-37979
                                       CIP

10 9 8 7 6 5 4 3 2 1

A Sterling/Chapelle Book

Published by Sterling Publishing Company, Inc.
387 Park Avenue South, New York, NY 10016
© 1997 by Chapelle Ltd.
Distributed in Canada by Sterling Publishing
c/o Canadian Manda Group, One Atlantic Avenue, Suite 105
Toronto, Ontario, Canada M6K 3E7
Distributed in Great Britain and Europe by Cassell PLC
Wellington House, 125 Strand, London WC2R 0BB, England
Distributed in Australia by Capricorn Link (Australia) Pty Ltd.
P.O. Box 6651, Baulkham Hills, Business Centre, NSW 2153, Australia
Printed in the United States

Sterling ISBN 0-8069-9341-3

Acknowledgements

Projects in this book were made
with products provided by the
following manufacturers:

Delta Ceramcoat Paints, DMC
Floss, Gay Bowles Mill Hill Beads
and Buttons, Jan Lynn, Kreinik,
C. M. Offray & Son, Inc., Utah
Frame, Wichelt Fabrics, and
Zweigart Fabrics

Pattern packets for dolls pictured on
pages 51, 55, and 113 are available
through Design Farm.

Patterns for Lori Gardner's wood
projects pictured throughout this book
can be found in the following Provo
Crafts' books: Checkerboard Farm,
Garden of Friends, and Heart & Souls.

If you have any questions or comments
or would like information about any
specialty products featured in this
book, please contact:

Chapelle Ltd., Inc.
P.O. Box 9252
Ogden, UT 84409

Phone: (801) 621-2777
FAX: (801) 621-2788

About the Author

Dedication
To my dear ones, Gregg, Madison, and Kennedy, with love and appreciation.

While every illustration Lori Gardner pens is a testament to her artistry, the real design credits often belong to a genius known as Mother Nature. And what an inspiration she's been. Lori spent her youth living on "the farm" in rural Blackfoot, Idaho, surrounded by horses, cows, rolling farmlands and a loving family. And, wherever Lori ventures, it is that experience which stirs her soul.

Lori has dabbled in every kind of design project imaginable. As a student of graphic design and illustration, she has been employed by several of Utah's top advertising agencies and has won recognition for her logos and creative compaigns. She decided she wanted to make a career out of what she already spent her nights, weekends and most of her life doing. Painting. She devoted her time to new projects inspired from the home-spun nostalgia of her childhood. Before long, painting heart-warming farm animals and country dolls blossomed into a full-time career.

Lori has also gained favor in several new mediums. She designs painting projects for books for Provo Crafts as well as projects for stencils, rub-ons, and transfers. She also creates fabric designs for MODA of United Notions and has a line of more than 150 rubber stamps. Her most recent venture, a fabric doll pattern packet series, appropriately named "Design Farm," has been featured on the covers of several national magazines.

Although painting, creating, and designing keep her busy, daughters, seven-year-old Madison and four-year-old Kennedy are really Lori's main focus in life. They can often be found at Lori's side with their own set of paper, pencils, and crayons. Her husband and business partner, Gregg, who has the glamourous task of duplicating, gluing, stuffing, and hand-addressing pattern packets for cutomers around the world—when he isn't at his post as a paramedic/firefighter for the City of Sandy, Utah Fire Department—is Lori's best friend and untiring inspiration. In her crazy world of deadlines, design pressures and unending telephone tasks, Lori still manages to escape into her studio to create her little piece of heaven with her brush and paper—forever inspired by heaven itself. "I live by the Amish prayer, 'My hands to work, my heart to God'," says Lori.

Contents

Acrylic Paints for Frames

We have matched Delta Ceramcoat acrylic paint names with generic color names.

Generic Color	Delta
Aqua-lt.	Salem Blue
Aqua-med.	Aquamarine
Beige-lt.	AC Flesh
Beige-vy. lt.	Oyster White
Brown-dk.	Territorial Beige
Brown-lt.	Trail Tan
Brown-med.	Golden Brown
Gold	Empire Gold
Gray-vy. dk.	Charcoal
Green-dk.	Alpine Green
Green-med.	Green Sea
Green Yellow-lt.	Wedgewood Green
Off White	Light Ivory
Orange	Pumpkin
Orange-dk.	Tangerine
Orange Yellow-lt.	Western Sunset
Pink-dk.	Lisa Pink
Pink-lt.	Pink Frosting
Pink-med.	Hydrangea Pink
Red-vy. dk.	Barn Red
Rose-dk.	Antique Rose
Rose-lt.	Indiana Rose
Rose-med.	Gypsy Rose
Rose-pale	Rose Cloud
Slate Blue	Liberty Blue
Slate Gray	Tide Pool Blue
Tan	Spice Tan
Tan-lt.	Maple Sugar
Tan-vy. lt.	Ivory
Yellow-lt.	Custard
Yellow-med.	Crocus Yellow

General Instructions

Fabric for Cross-stitch

Counted cross-stitch is usually worked on even-weave fabrics. These fabrics are manufactured specifically for counted-thread embroidery and are woven with the same number of vertical as horizontal threads per inch.

Preparing Fabric

Cut fabric at least 3" larger on all sides than finished design size to ensure space for desired assembly. To prevent fraying, machine-zigzag or whipstitch edges or apply liquid fray preventer.

Needles for Cross-stitch

For fabric with 11 or fewer threads per inch, use a tapestry needle size 24; for 14 threads per inch, use a size 24 or 26; for 18 or more threads per inch, use a size 26. Never leave needle in fabric.

Floss

Use 18" lengths of floss. For best coverage, separate strands. Dampen with wet sponge. Then put together number of strands required.

Centering the Design

Fold fabric in half horizontally, then vertically. Place a pin at fold point to mark center. Locate center of design as indicated by arrows centered left and bottom on each graph. Begin stitching at center of graph and fabric.

Securing the Floss

Insert needle up from underside of fabric at starting point. Hold 1" of thread behind fabric and stitch over it, securing with the first few stitches. To finish thread, run under four or more stitches on back of design. Never knot floss, unless working on clothing.

Carrying Floss

To carry floss, weave floss under previously worked stitches on back. Do not carry thread across any fabric that is not or will not be stitched. Loose threads, especially those that are dark, will show through the fabric.

Cleaning Completed Work

When stitching is complete, soak fabric in cold water with a mild soap for five to 10 minutes. Rinse well and roll in a towel to remove excess water. Do not wring. Place work face down on a dry towel and iron on warm setting until the fabric is dry.

Cross-stitch

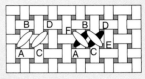

Stitches are done in a row or, if necessary, one at a time in an area. Stitching is done by coming up through a hole between woven threads at A. Then, go down diagonally at B. Come back up at C and down at D, etc. Complete the top stitches to create an "X". All top stitches should lie in same direction. Come up at E and go down at B, come up at C and go down at F, etc.

Backstitch

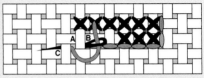

Pull needle through at point marked A. Go down one opening to the right, at B. Then, come back up at C. Now, go down one opening to the right, this time at "A". Continue in this manner.

French Knot

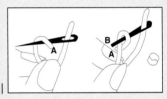

Bring needle up at A. Loosely wrap floss once around needle. Place needle at B, next to A. Pull floss taut while pushing needle down through fabric. Carry floss across back of work between knots.

Lazy Daisy

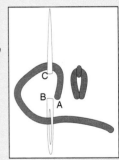

Bring needle up at A. Put needle down through fabric at B and up through at C, keeping thread under needle to form a loop. Pull thread through, leaving loop loose and full. To hold loop in place, go down on other side of thread near C, forming a straight stitch over loop.

Long Stitch

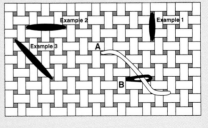

Bring needle up at A; go down at B. Pull flat. Repeat A–B for each stitch. Length of the stitch should be the same as line length on design chart. This stitch can be horizontal, vertical, or diagonal.

Spring

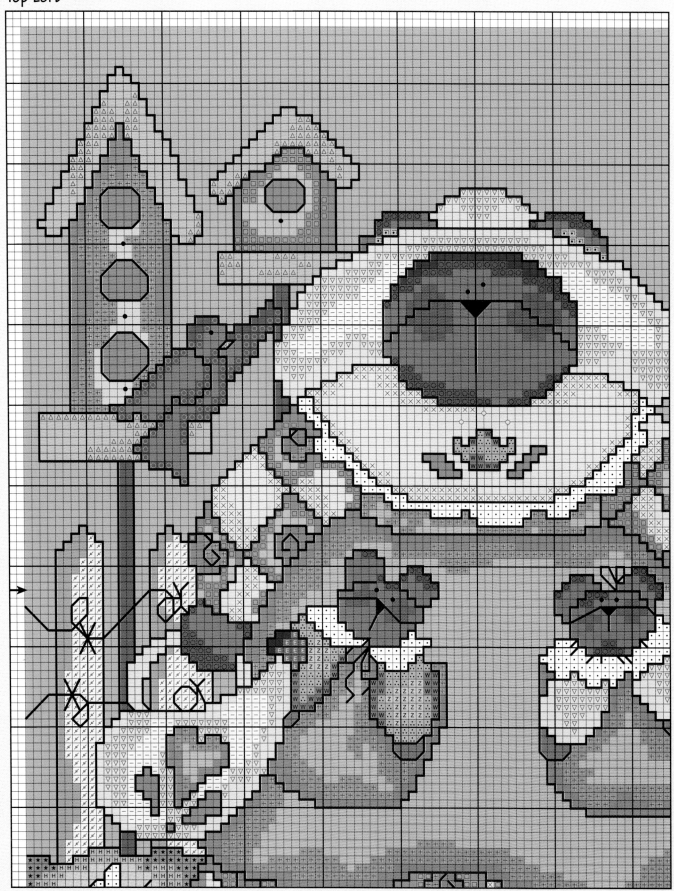

Pockets Full Of Bearsies

Sample Information
The sample was stitched on white Belfast linen 32 over two threads. The finished design size is 7¼" x 8¾". The fabric was cut 14" x 15".

Stitch Count: 116 x 140

Other Fabrics	Finished Size
Aida 11	10½" x 12¾"
Aida 14	8¼" x 10"
Aida 18	6½" x 7¾"
Hardanger 22	5¼" x 6⅜"

Frame Finishing
Colors used for painting the frame are Pink–med., Green Yellow–lt., Rose–med., and Orange Yellow–lt. Also used was a .25 permanent black lining pen.

Anchor		DMC	

Step 1: Cross Stitch (2 strands)

Anchor		DMC	
1	· ⁄		White
387		712	Cream
386	– –	746	Off White
300	▽ ▽	745	Yellow–lt. pale
301		744	Yellow–pale
48		818	Baby Pink
24		776	Pink–med. (1 strand)
25	+ ⁄	3326	Rose–lt.
27		899	Rose–med.
894		223	Shell Pink–med.
117		341	Blue Violet–lt.
118	◎ ⊘	340	Blue Violet–med.
119		3746	Blue Violet–dk.
158	Z	775	Baby Blue–vy. lt.
128	∴ ⁄	800	Delft–pale
128		800	Delft–pale (1 strand)
130	W	809	Delft
213		369	Pistachio Green–vy. lt.
214	H	368	Pistachio Green–lt.
215	★	320	Pistachio Green–med.
213		504	Blue Green–lt.
875	□	503	Blue Green–med.
876	■	502	Blue Green
387	⁄	822	Beige Gray–lt.
899		3782	Mocha Brown–lt.
885	X	739	Tan–ultra vy. lt.

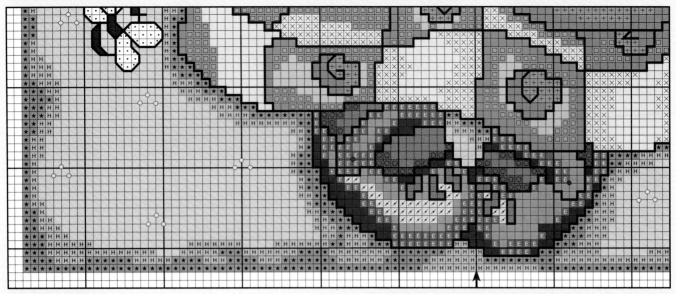

Bottom Left

362	437	Tan–lt.
363	436	Tan
309	435	Brown–vy. lt.
933	3774	Peach Pecan–med.
882	407	Pecan
914	3772	Pecan–med.
936	632	Pecan–dk.
397	762	Pearl Gray–vy. lt.
398	415	Pearl Gray
400	414	Steel Gray–dk.
401	413	Pewter Gray–dk.
403	310	Black

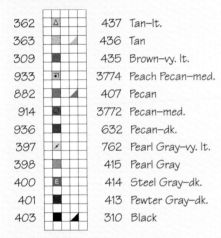

Step 2: Backstitch (1 strand)

403   310   Black

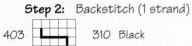

Step 3: French Knot (1 strand)

403   310   Black

Step 4: Beads

○   00128   Yellow

●   00081   Jet

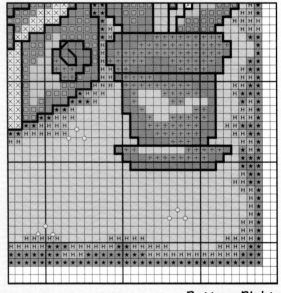

Bottom Right

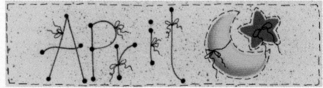

11

Easter Bunnies

Sample Information

The sample was stitched on white Cashel linen 28 over two threads. The finished design size is 11½" x 7⅞". The fabric was cut 18" x 14".

Stitch Count: 161 x 99

Other Fabrics	Finished Size
Aida 11	14⅝" x 9"
Aida 18	9" x 5½"
Hardanger 22	7⅜" x 4½"

Anchor		DMC	

Step 1: Cross Stitch (2 strands)

892		3770	Peach Pecan-vy. lt.
881		945	Peach Beige
882		3773	Pecan-vy. lt.
8		761	Salmon-lt.
9		760	Salmon
11		3328	Salmon-dk.
975		3753	Antique Blue-ultra vy. lt.
920		932	Antique Blue-lt.
921		931	Antique Blue-med.
217		3817	Celadon Green-lt.
876		3816	Celadon Green
403		310	Black

Step 2: Backstitch (1 strand)

11		3328	Salmon-dk.
876		3816	Celadon Green
403		310	Black

Step 3: French Knot (1 strand)

403		310	Black

Step 3: Beads

		00525	Light Green

Frame Finishing

Colors used for painting the frame are Slate Gray, Off White, and Rose-pale. Also used was a .25 permanent black lining pen.

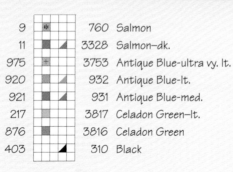

14

Sweet & Simple

Sample Information

The sample was stitched on green Dublin 28 over two threads. The finished design size is 10¾" x 15⅛". The fabric was cut 17" x 22".

Stitch Count: 151 x 211

Other Fabrics	Finished Size
Aida 11	13¾" x 19⅛"
Aida 18	8⅜" x 11¾"
Hardanger 22	6⅞" x 9⅝"

Anchor		DMC	

Step 1: Cross Stitch (2 strands)

Anchor		DMC	
886		677	Old Gold–vy. lt.
891		676	Old Gold–lt.
890		729	Old Gold–med.
1047		3825	Pumpkin–pale
323	Z	722	Orange Spice–lt.
324		721	Orange Spice–med.
892		225	Shell Pink–vy. lt.
893		224	Shell Pink–lt.
894		223	Shell Pink–med.
896		3721	Shell Pink–dk.
25		3326	Rose–lt.
27	W	899	Rose–med.
42		335	Rose
975		3753	Antique Blue–ultra vy. lt.
920	+	932	Antique Blue–lt.
921		931	Antique Blue–med.
217		3817	Celadon Green–lt.
876	▽	3816	Celadon Green
877		3815	Celadon Green–dk.
213		369	Pistachio Green–vy. lt.
214	P	368	Pistachio Green–lt.
216		367	Pistachio Green–dk.
942		738	Tan–vy. lt.
362		437	Tan–lt. (1 strand)
363	✓	436	Tan (1 strand)

Step 2: Backstitch (1 strand)

Anchor		DMC	
896		3721	Shell Pink–dk.
324		721	Orange Spice–med.
921		931	Antique Blue–med.
877		3815	Celadon Green–dk.
216		367	Pistachio Green–dk.
403		310	Black

Step 3: French Knot (1 strand)

Anchor		DMC	
403	•	310	Black

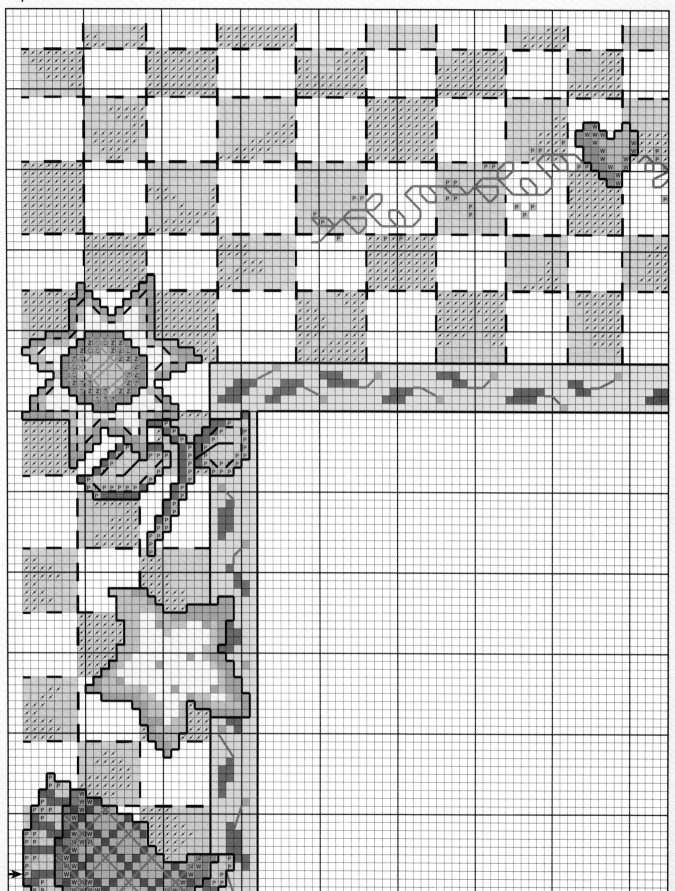

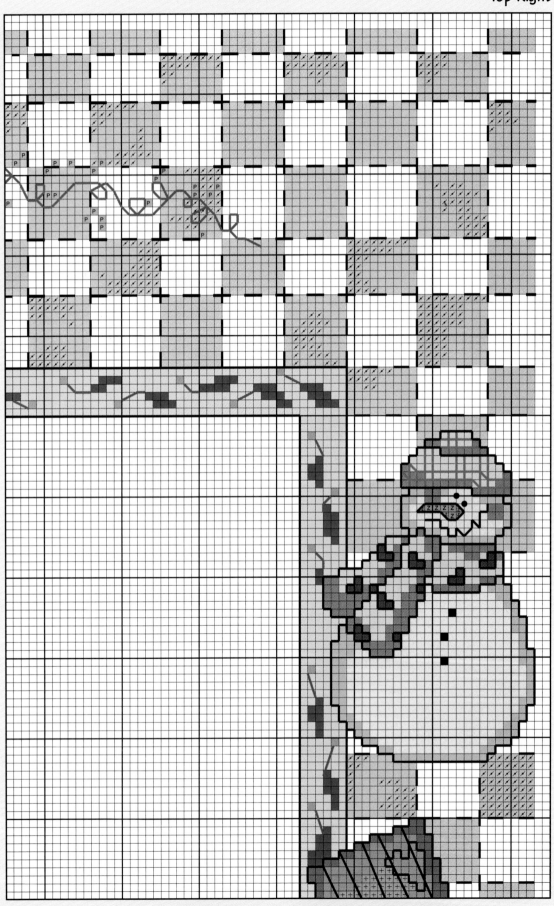

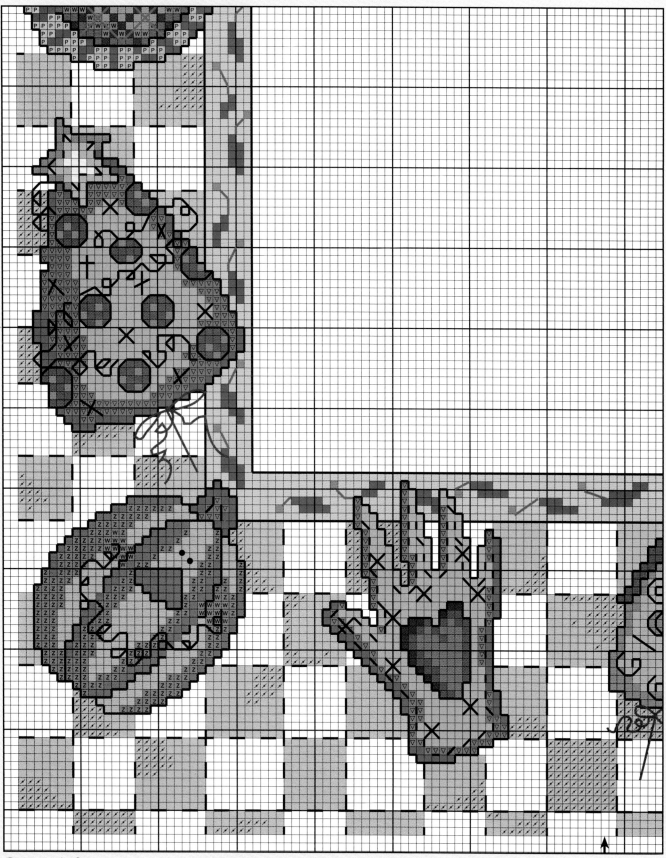

Bottom Left

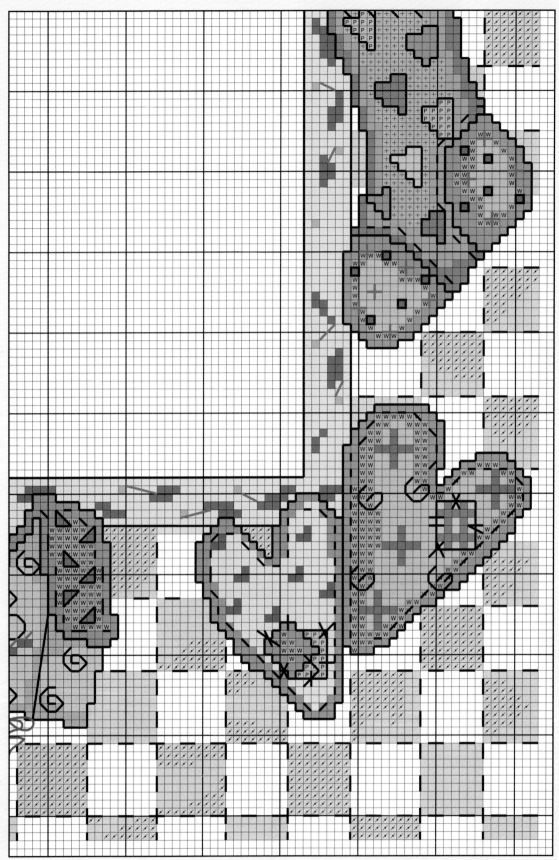

Bottom Right

Up, Up & Away

Sample Information

The sample was stitched on ice blue Jubilee 28 over two threads. The finished design size is 2⅛" x 7½". The fabric was cut 9" x 14".

Stitch Count: 29 x 105

Other Fabrics	Finished Size
Aida 11	2⅝" x 9½"
Aida 18	1⅝" x 5⅞"
Hardanger 22	1⅜" x 4¾"

Anchor   DMC

Step 1: Cross Stitch (2 strands)

Anchor		DMC	
386		746	Off White
886		677	Old Gold–vy. lt.
891		676	Old Gold–lt.
48		818	Baby Pink
25		3326	Rose–lt.
27		899	Rose–med.
893		224	Shell Pink–lt.
894		223	Shell Pink–med.
896		3721	Shell Pink–dk.
975		3753	Antique Blue–ultra vy. lt.
920		932	Antique Blue–lt.
921		931	Antique Blue–med.
213		504	Blue Green–lt.
217		3817	Celadon Green–lt.
876		3816	Celadon Green
942		738	Tan–vy. lt.
363		436	Tan
376		842	Beige Brown–vy. lt.
378		841	Beige Brown–lt.
379		840	Beige Brown–med.
403		310	Black

Step 2: Backstitch (1 strand)

Anchor		DMC	
403		310	Black

Step 3: Long Stitch (1 strand)

Anchor		DMC	
891		676	Old Gold–lt.
27		899	Rose–med.
896		3721	Shell Pink–dk.
922		930	Antique Blue–dk.
363		436	Tan
403		310	Black

Step 4: French Knot (1 strand)

Anchor		DMC	
886		677	Old Gold–vy. lt.
891		676	Old Gold–lt.
894		223	Shell Pink–med.
876		3816	Celadon Green
403		310	Black

Step 5: Lazy Daisy (1 strand)

Anchor		DMC	
403		310	Black

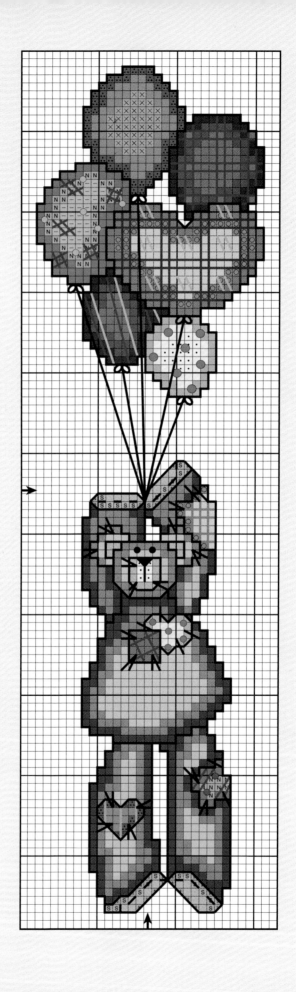

Flowers to Thee

Sample Information
The sample was stitched on carnation Pastel linen 28 over two threads. The finished design size is 5⅝" x 12". The fabric was cut 12" x 18".

Stitch Count: 78 x 168

Other Fabrics
Aida 11
Aida 18
Hardanger 22

Finished Size
7⅛" x 15¼"
4⅜" x 9⅜"
3½" x 7⅝"

Frame Finishing
Colors used for painting the frame are Beige—vy. lt. and Rose—pale.

Step 1: Cross Stitch (2 strands)

292		3078	Golden Yellow–vy. lt.
907	+	3822	Straw–lt.
306		3820	Straw–dk.
25		3326	Rose–lt.
27		899	Rose–med.
892		225	Shell Pink–vy. lt.
893		224	Shell Pink–lt.
894		223	Shell Pink–med.
975		3753	Antique Blue–ultra vy. lt.
264		772	Pine Green–lt.
265		3348	Yellow Green–lt.
266		3347	Yellow Green–med.
324	z	922	Copper–lt.
339		920	Copper–med.

933		3774	Peach Pecan–med.
4146	·	950	Peach Pecan–dk.
942		738	Tan–vy. lt.
376	◎ ◹	842	Beige Brown–vy. lt.
378	△	841	Beige Brown–lt.
379		840	Beige Brown–med.

Step 2: Backstitch (1 strand)

265		3348	Yellow Green–lt.
403		310	Black

Step 3: French Knot (1 strand)

403	•	310	Black

Flowers To Thee

Top

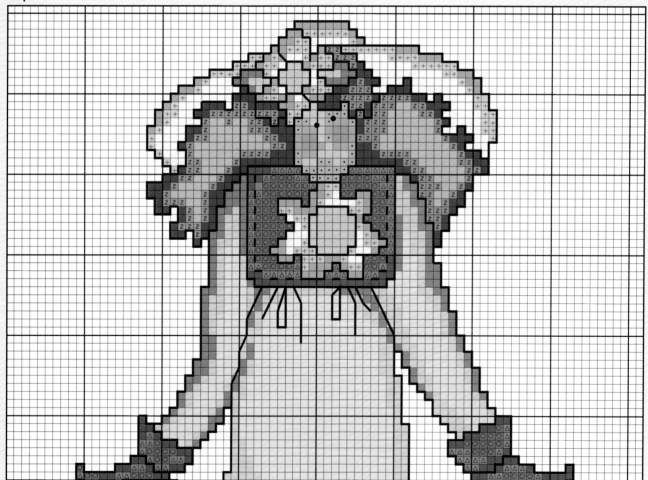

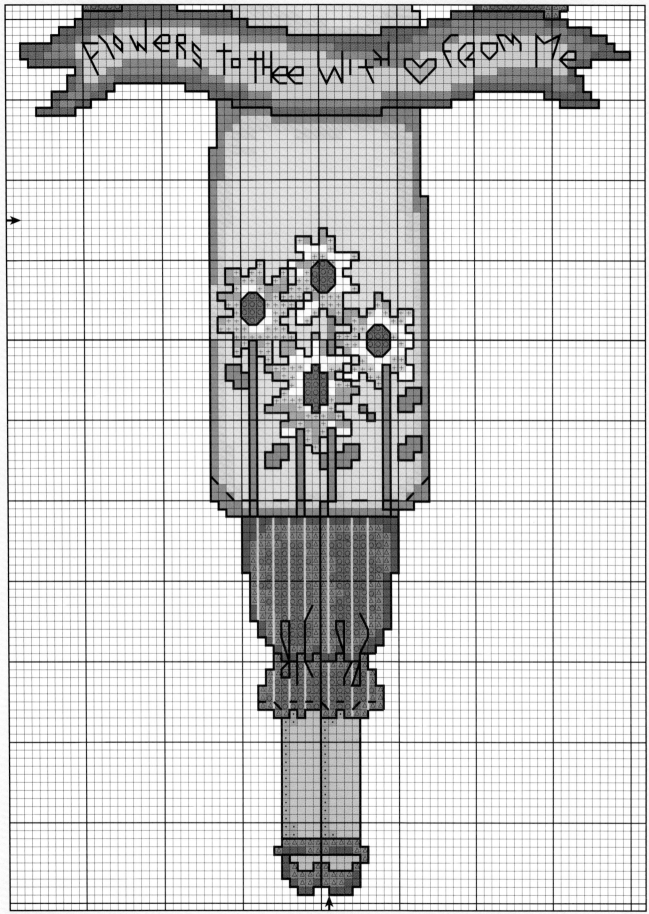

Bottom

Blue Bow

Stitch Count: 58 x 54

Fabrics	Finished Size
Aida 11	5¼" x 4⅞"
Aida 14	4⅛" x 3⅞"
Aida 18	3¼" x 3"
Hardanger 22	2⅝" x 2½"

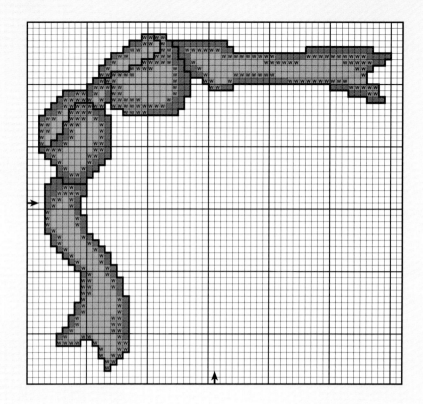

Anchor   DMC

Step 1: Cross Stitch (2 strands)

975		3753 Antique Blue–ultra vy. lt.
920	W	932 Antique Blue–lt.
921		931 Antique Blue–med.

Step 2: Backstitch (1 strand)

403		310 Black

Garden Gloves

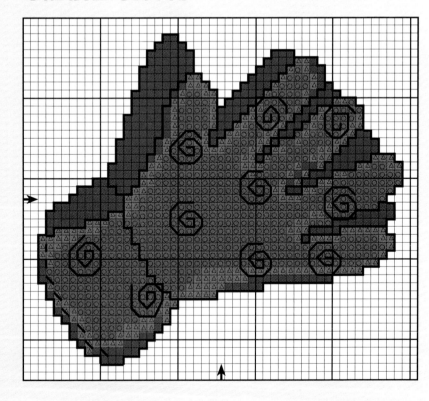

Stitch Count: 47 x 41

Fabrics	Finished Size
Aida 11	4¼" x 3¾"
Aida 14	3⅜" x 2⅞"
Aida 18	2⅝" x 2¼"
Hardanger 22	2⅛" x 1⅞"

Anchor   DMC

Step 1: Cross Stitch (2 strands)

376		842 Beige Brown–vy. lt.
378		841 Beige Brown–lt.
379		840 Beige Brown–med.

Step 2: Backstitch (1 strand)

403		310 Black

Tall Birdhouse

Stitch Count: 20 x 62

Fabrics	Finished Size
Aida 11	1⅞" x 5⅝"
Aida 14	1⅜" x 4½"
Aida 18	1⅛" x 3½"
Hardanger 22	⅞" x 2⅞"

Anchor   DMC

Step 1: Cross Stitch (2 strands)

Anchor	DMC	
926		Ecru
892	225	Shell Pink–vy. lt.
893	224	Shell Pink–lt.
975	3753	Antique Blue–ultra vy. lt.
920	932	Antique Blue–lt.
921	931	Antique Blue–med.

Step 2: Backstitch (1 strand)

403	310 Black

Step 3: French Knot (1 strand)

403	310 Black

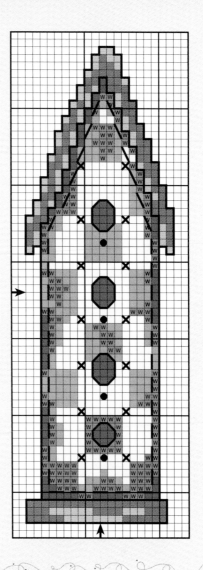

Short Birdhouse

Stitch Count: 28 x 31

Fabrics	Finished Size
Aida 11	2½" x 2⅞"
Aida 14	2" x 2¼"
Aida 18	1½" x 1¾"
Hardanger 22	1¼" x 1⅜"

Anchor   DMC

Step 3: French Knot (1 strand)

403	310 Black

Step 1: Cross Stitch (2 strands)

Anchor	DMC	
926		Ecru
27	899	Rose–med.
42	335	Rose
59	326	Rose–vy. dk.
376	842	Beige Brown–vy. lt.
378	841	Beige Brown–lt.

Step 2: Backstitch (1 strand)

403	310 Black

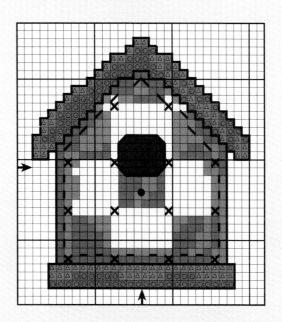

Single Sunflower

Dress Finishing

Motifs below and on page 30 are stitched on a white cotton dress using waste canvas 14. The canvas for the Bodice Left Motif is cut 4" x 4". The canvas for the Skirt Motifs is cut in three 8" x 4" pieces. Motifs are spaced evenly across skirt.

Bodice Left Motif

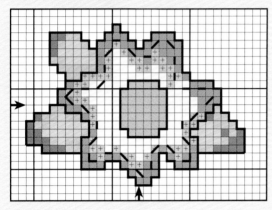

Stitch Count: 29 x 20

Fabrics	Finished Size
Aida 11	2⅝" x 1⅞"
Aida 14	2⅛" x 1⅜"
Aida 18	1⅝" x 1⅛"
Hardanger 22	1⅜" x ⅞"

Anchor		DMC	

Step 1: Cross Stitch (2 strands)

292		3078	Golden Yellow—vy. lt.
907	+	3822	Straw—lt.
306		3820	Straw—dk.
264		772	Pine Green—lt.
265		3348	Yellow Green—lt.
266		3347	Yellow Green—med.
942		738	Tan—vy. lt.
363		436	Tan

Step 2: Backstitch (1 strand)

403		310	Black

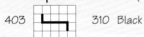

Garden Trowel

Stitch Count: 44 x 27

Fabrics	Finished Size
Aida 11	4" x 2½"
Aida 14	3⅛" x 1⅞"
Aida 18	2½" x 1½"
Hardanger 22	2" x 1¼"

Skirt Motif

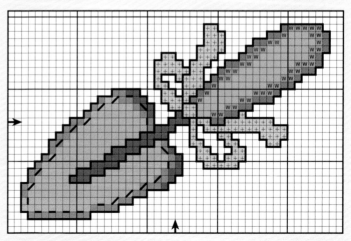

Anchor   DMC

Step 1:		Cross Stitch (2 strands)	
907	+	3822	Straw–lt.
975		3753	Antique Blue–ultra vy. lt.
920	w	932	Antique Blue–lt.
921		931	Antique Blue–med.
397		453	Shell Gray–lt.
398		452	Shell Gray–med.
399		451	Shell Gray–dk.

Step 2:		Backstitch (1 strand)	
403		310	Black

Stitch Count: 20 x 50

Fabrics	Finished Size
Aida 11	1⅞" x 4½"
Aida 14	1⅜" x 3⅝"
Aida 18	1⅛" x 2¾"
Hardanger 22	⅞" x 2¼"

Optional Motif Direction

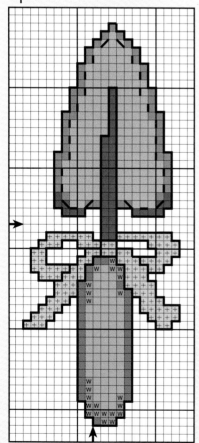

Sunflower Chain

Stitch Count: 40 x 61

Fabrics	Finished Size
Aida 11	3⅝" x 5½"
Aida 14	2⅞" x 4⅜"
Aida 18	2¼" x 3⅜"
Hardanger 22	1⅞" x 2¾"

Optional Motif Direction

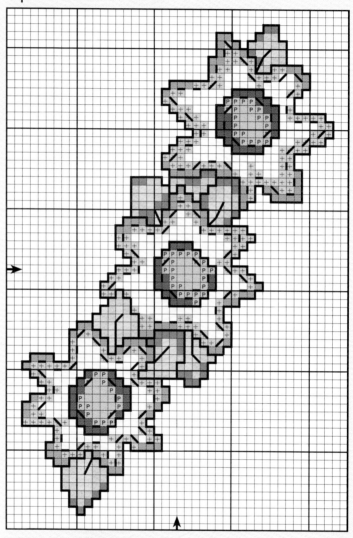

Anchor   DMC

Step 1:		Cross Stitch (2 strands)	
292		3078	Golden Yellow–vy. lt.
907	+	3822	Straw–lt.
306		3820	Straw–dk.
264		772	Pine Green–lt.
265		3348	Yellow Green–lt.
266		3347	Yellow Green–med.
942		738	Tan–vy. lt.

363		436	Tan
370		434	Brown–lt.

Step 2: Backstitch (1 strand)

403		310	Black

Stitch Count: 69 x 21

Fabrics	Finished Size
Aida 11	6¼" x 1⅞"
Aida 14	4⅞" x 1½"
Aida 18	3⅞" x 1⅛"
Hardanger 22	3⅛" x 1"

Skirt Motif

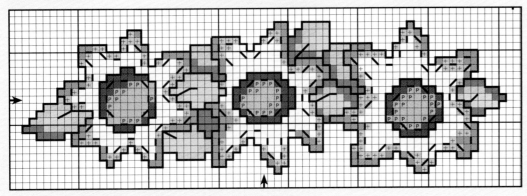

Watering Can

Stitch Count: 36 x 27

Fabrics	Finished Size
Aida 11	3¼" x 2½"
Aida 14	2⅝" x 1⅞"
Aida 18	2" x 1½"
Hardanger 22	1⅝" x 1¼"

Skirt Motif

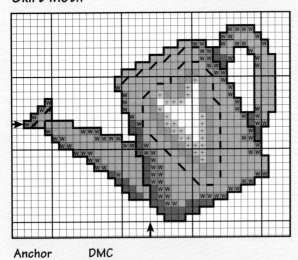

Anchor	DMC

Step 1: Cross Stitch (2 strands)

292		3078	Golden Yellow–vy. lt.
907	+	3822	Straw–lt.
306		3820	Straw–dk.

975		3753	Antique Blue–ultra vy. lt.
920	W	932	Antique Blue–lt.
921		931	Antique Blue–med.

Step 2: Backstitch (1 strand)

403		310	Black

Stitch Count: 38 x 25

Fabrics	Finished Size
Aida 11	3½" x 2¼"
Aida 14	2¾" x 1¾"
Aida 18	2⅛" x 1⅜"
Hardanger 22	1¾" x 1⅛"

Optional Motif Direction

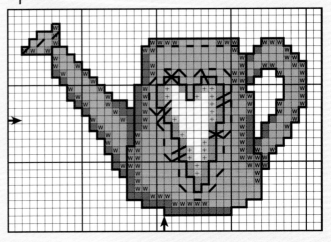

Spring Quilt

Sample Information
The sample was stitched on antique lavender linen 28 over two threads. The finished design size is 10¼" x 7⅝". The fabric was cut 17" x 14".

Stitch Count: 143 x 106

Other Fabrics	Finished Size
Aida 11	13" x 9⅝"
Aida 18	8" x 5⅞"
Hardanger 22	6½" x 4⅞"

Anchor	DMC	

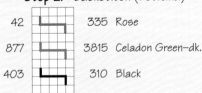

Step 1: Cross Stitch (2 strands)

Anchor		DMC	
			White
886		677	Old Gold–vy. lt.
891		676	Old Gold–lt.
6		3824	Apricot–lt.
328		3341	Apricot
48		818	Baby Pink
24		776	Pink–med.
27		899	Rose–med.
42		335	Rose
975		3753	Antique Blue–ultra vy. lt.
920	W w	932	Antique Blue–lt.
921		931	Antique Blue–med.
217		3817	Celadon Green–lt.
876		3816	Celadon Green
877		3815	Celadon Green–dk.
387		712	Cream
942		738	Tan–vy. lt.
363	P P	435	Tan

Step 2: Backstitch (1 strand)

Anchor	DMC	
42	335	Rose
877	3815	Celadon Green–dk.
403	310	Black

Step 3: Lazy Daisy (1 strand)

Anchor	DMC	
877	3815	Celadon Green–dk.

Step 4: French Knot (1 strand)

Anchor	DMC	
		White
42	335	Rose
403	310	Black

Step 5: Button

		White Bird-shaped

Frame Finishing
Colors used for painting the frame are Green–med., Rose–pale, Rose–dk., and Green–dk. Also used was a .25 permanent black lining pen.

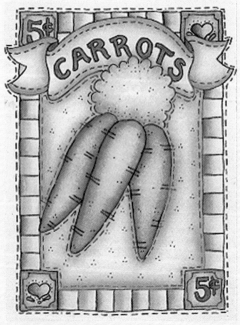

My garden is the
I like to be;
The birds and bunr
keep me compan
While friendships b
around me.

Heaven Sent

Sample Information

The sample was stitched on lt. terra cotta Lugana 25 over two threads. The finished design size is 8⅜" x 11⅝". The fabric was cut 15" x 18".

Stitch Count: 105 x 145

Other Fabrics	Finished Size
Aida 11	9½" x 13⅛"
Aida 14	7½" x 10⅜"
Aida 18	5⅞" x 8⅛"
Hardanger 22	4¾" x 6⅝"

Frame Finishing

Colors used for painting the frame are Yellow—lt., Rose—dk., Slate Gray, and Green—med.

Anchor   DMC

Step 1: Cross Stitch (2 strands)

Anchor			DMC	
386	△	△	746	Off White
886			677	Old Gold–vy. lt.
891			676	Old Gold–lt.
4146			754	Peach–lt.
8			761	Salmon–lt.
9	W	w	760	Salmon
11			3328	Salmon–dk.
893			224	Shell Pink–lt.
894	R		223	Shell Pink–med.
896			3721	Shell Pink–dk.
975			3753	Antique Blue–ultra vy. lt.
920	+		932	Antique Blue–lt.
921			931	Antique Blue–med.
922	▩		930	Antique Blue–dk.
928			598	Turquoise–lt.
167			597	Turquoise
1039			3810	Turquoise–dk.
213			369	Pistachio Green–vy. lt.
214	✗		368	Pistachio Green–lt.
215			320	Pistachio Green–med.
387			712	Cream
942	z	z	738	Tan–vy. lt.
363			436	Tan
309			435	Brown–vy. lt.

Step 2: Backstitch (1 strand)

Anchor		DMC	
1			White
11		3328	Salmon–dk.
896		3721	Shell Pink–dk.
167		597	Turquoise
1039		3810	Turquoise–dk.
403		310	Black

Step 3: French Knot (1 strand)

Anchor		DMC	
891	○	676	Old Gold–lt.
11	●	3328	Salmon–dk.
896	●	3721	Shell Pink–dk.
1039	●	3810	Turquoise–dk.
387	○	712	Cream
403	●	310	Black

Alphabet Top

Alphabet Bottom Left

Alphabet Bottom Right

36

Heaven Sent

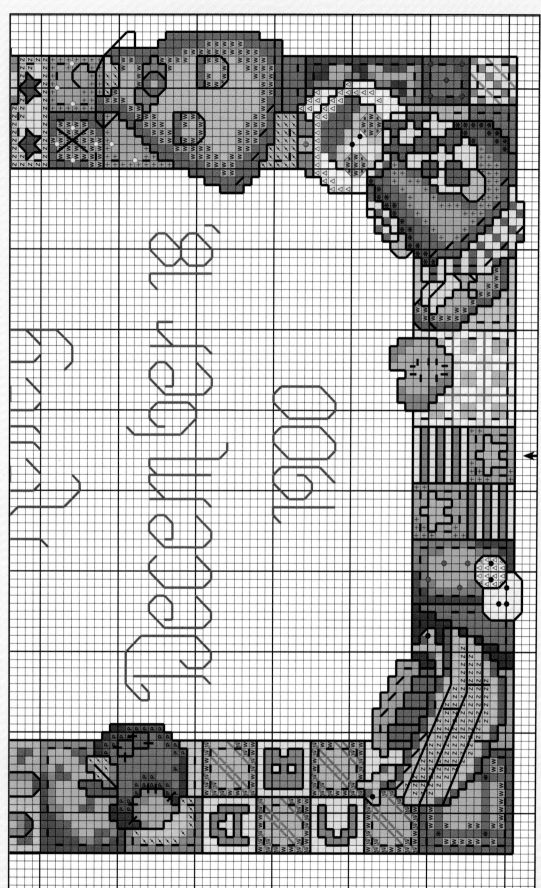

December 18, 1900

Summer

Plant your seeds in a row.
One for the pheasant,
One for the crow.
One to rot and one to grow.

our seeds in a row

for the pheasant,

for the crow.

ot and one to gro

Plant Your Seeds

Sample Information

The sample was stitched on ivory Belfast linen 32 over two threads. The finished design size is 13⅝" x 8½". The fabric was cut 20" x 15".

Stitch Count: 217 x 136

Other Fabrics	Finished Size
Aida 11	19¾" x 12⅜"
Aida 14	15½" x 9¾"
Aida 18	12" x 7½"
Hardanger 22	9⅞" x 6⅛"

Anchor			DMC	

Step 1: Cross Stitch (2 strands)

Anchor		DMC	Color
387		712	Cream
386		746	Off White
292		3078	Golden Yellow—vy. lt.
301		744	Yellow—pale
886		677	Old Gold—vy. lt.
891		676	Old Gold—lt.
890		729	Old Gold—med.
323		722	Orange Spice—lt.
324		721	Orange Spice—med.
326		720	Orange Spice—dk.
328		3341	Apricot
11		3328	Salmon—dk.
271		3713	Salmon—vy. lt.
8		761	Salmon—lt.
9		760	Salmon
24		776	Pink—med.
27		899	Rose—med.
42		335	Rose
158		775	Baby Blue—vy. lt.
128		800	Delft—pale
154		3755	Baby Blue
975		3753	Antique Blue—ultra vy. lt.
920		932	Antique Blue—lt.
921		931	Antique Blue—med.
213		369	Pistachio Green—vy. lt.
214		368	Pistachio Green—lt.
215		320	Pistachio Green—med.
216		367	Pistachio Green—dk.
942		738	Tan—vy. lt.
362		437	Tan—lt.
363		436	Tan
309		435	Brown—vy. lt.

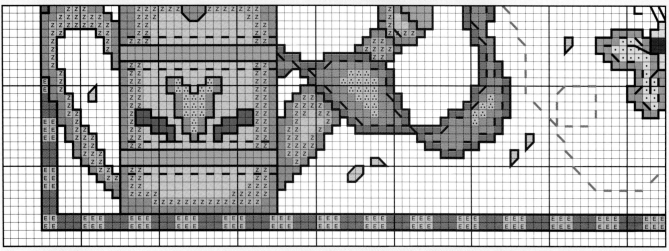

Bottom Left

Bottom Middle

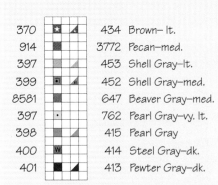

370	★	◢	434	Brown– lt.
914			3772	Pecan–med.
397		◢	453	Shell Gray–lt.
399	•◢	◢	452	Shell Gray–med.
8581			647	Beaver Gray–med.
397	•		762	Pearl Gray–vy. lt.
398		◢	415	Pearl Gray
400	W		414	Steel Gray–dk.
401		◢	413	Pewter Gray–dk.

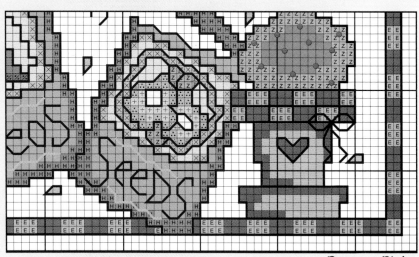

Bottom Right

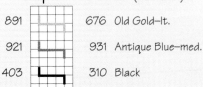

Step 2: Backstitch (1 strand)

891		676	Old Gold–lt.
921		931	Antique Blue–med.
403		310	Black

Step 3: French Knot (1 strand)

11	•	3328	Salmon–dk.
921	•	931	Antique Blue–med.
216	•	367	Pistachio Green–dk.
370	•	434	Brown– lt.
403	•	310	Black

Frame Finishing

Colors used for painting the frame are Green Yellow–lt., Green–dk., and Orange. Also used was a .25 permanent black lining pen.

Welcome Friends

Sample Information

The sample was stitched on white Glasgow linen 28 over two threads. The finished design size is 8¼" x 9⅛". The fabric was cut 15" x 16".

Stitch Count: 116 x 127

Other Fabrics	Finished Size
Aida 11	10½" x 11½"
Aida 18	6½" x 7"
Hardanger 22	5¼" x 5¾"

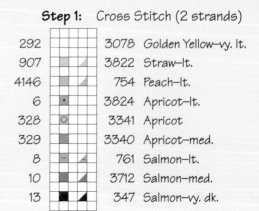

Anchor		DMC	
Step 1:		Cross Stitch (2 strands)	
292		3078	Golden Yellow–vy. lt.
907		3822	Straw–lt.
4146		754	Peach–lt.
6	·	3824	Apricot–lt.
328	○	3341	Apricot
329		3340	Apricot–med.
8	–	761	Salmon–lt.
10		3712	Salmon–med.
13		347	Salmon–vy. dk.

44

158	775	Baby Blue–vy. lt.
159	3325	Baby Blue–lt.
154	3755	Baby Blue
978	322	Navy Blue–vy. lt.
213	369	Pistachio Green–vy. lt.
214	368	Pistachio Green–lt.
215	320	Pistachio Green–med.
942	738	Tan–vy. lt.
363	436	Tan
309	435	Brown–vy. lt.
371	433	Brown–med.

Step 2: Backstitch (1 strand)

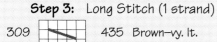

907	3822	Straw–lt.
13	347	Salmon–vy. dk.
978	322	Navy Blue–vy. lt.
215	320	Pistachio Green–med. (2 strands)
371	433	Brown–med.
		Gold Metallic
403	310	Black

Step 3: Long Stitch (1 strand)

| 309 | 435 | Brown–vy. lt. |

Step 4: French Knot (1 strand)

| 371 | 433 | Brown–med. |
| 403 | 310 | Black |

Step 5: Lazy Daisy (1 strand)

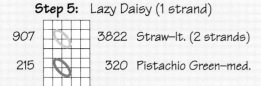

| 907 | 3822 | Straw–lt. (2 strands) |
| 215 | 320 | Pistachio Green–med. |

Frame Finishing

Colors used for painting the frame are Slate Gray, Off White, Slate Blue, Green Yellow–lt., Orange, and Orange–dk. Also used was a .25 permanent black lining pen.

Welcome Friends
Top Left

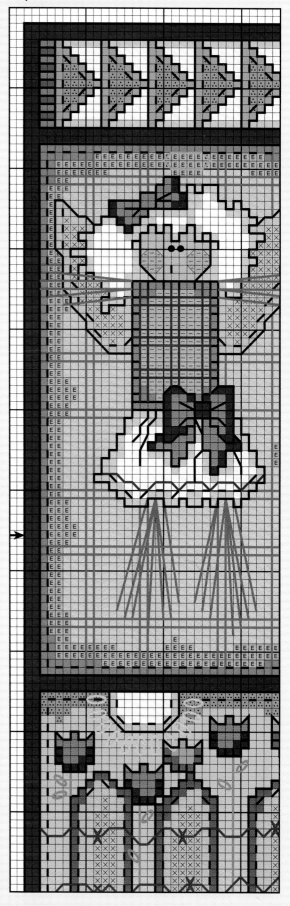

Top Right

Welcome
friends, Angels,
Cats, Sunshine,
Birds, All!
Butterflies

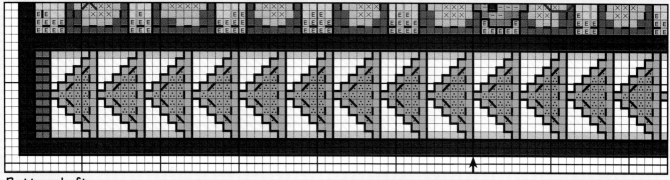

Bottom Left

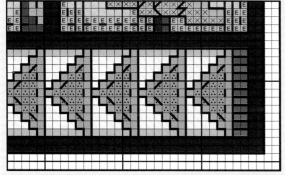

Bottom Right

Carrot Bunch

Stitch Count: 39 x 60

Fabrics	Finished Size
Aida 11	3½" x 5½"
Aida 14	2¾" x 4¼"
Aida 18	2⅛" x 3⅜"
Hardanger 22	1¾" x 2¾"

Anchor		DMC	

Step 1: Cross Stitch (2 strands)

1047		3825	Pumpkin–pale
323		722	Orange Spice–lt.
324		721	Orange Spice–med.
264		772	Pine Green–lt.
265		3348	Yellow Green–lt.
208		563	Jade–lt.

Step 2: Backstitch (1 strand)

403		310	Black

Garden Of Love

Sample Information

The sample was stitched on blue Amsterdam 16. The finished design size is 9" x 6½". The fabric was cut 15" x 13".

Stitch Count: 145 x 103

Other Fabrics
Aida 11
Aida 14
Aida 18
Hardanger 22

Finished Size
13⅛" x 9⅜"
10⅜" x 7⅜"
8⅛" x 5¾"
6⅝" x 4⅝"

Frame Finishing

Colors used for painting the frame are Slate Gray, Tan—vy. lt., and Brown—lt. Also used was a .25 permanent black lining pen.

Garden of Love

Left

Anchor		DMC	

Step 1: Cross Stitch (2 strands)

Anchor	DMC	
386	746	Off White
886	677	Old Gold–vy. lt.
891	676	Old Gold–lt.
4146	754	Peach–lt.
8	761	Salmon–lt.
10	3712	Salmon–med.
13	347	Salmon–vy. dk.
158	775	Baby Blue–vy. lt.
159	3325	Baby Blue–lt.
154	3755	Baby Blue
978	322	Navy Blue–vy. lt.
213	369	Pistachio Green–vy. lt.
214	368	Pistachio Green–lt.
215	320	Pistachio Green–med.
942	738	Tan–vy. lt.
362	437	Tan–lt.
363	436	Tan
309	435	Brown–vy. lt.
370	434	Brown– lt.
371	433	Brown–med.
387	822	Beige Gray–lt.
830	644	Beige Gray–med.
392	642	Beige Gray–dk.

Step 2: Backstitch (1 strand)

Anchor	DMC	
978	322	Navy Blue–vy. lt.
215	320	Pistachio Green–med.
879	890	Pistachio Green–ultra dk.
309	435	Brown–vy. lt.
403	310	Black

Step 3: French Knot (1 strand)

403	310	Black

Step 4: Ribbon

Green 4mm

Step 5: Buttons

Assorted Bird-shaped

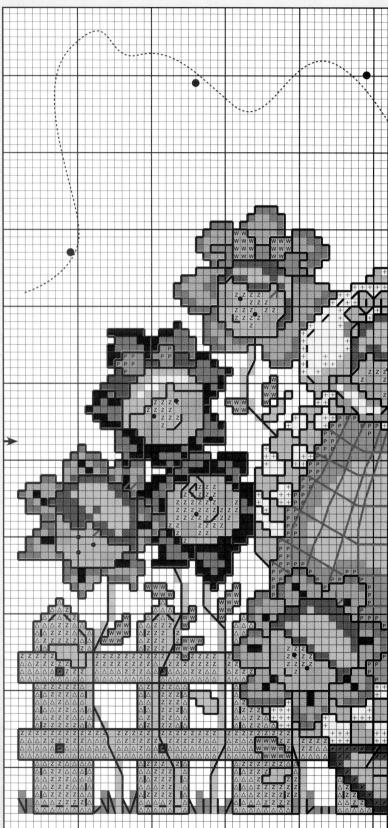

Lucy Locket

Sample Information
The sample was stitched on mint green Jubilee 28 over two threads. The finished design size is 12⅛" x 6¾". The fabric was cut 19" x 13".

Stitch Count: 169 x 95

Other Fabrics	Finished Size
Aida 11	15⅜" x 8⅝"
Aida 18	9⅜" x 5¼"
Hardanger 22	7⅝" x 4⅜"

Anchor	DMC	

Step 1: Cross Stitch (2 strands)

Anchor		DMC	
387		712	Cream
886		677	Old Gold–vy. lt.
891		676	Old Gold–lt.
366		951	Peach Pecan–lt.
324		922	Copper–lt.
349		921	Copper
339		920	Copper–med.
892	P	225	Shell Pink–vy. lt.
9		760	Salmon
49		3689	Mauve–lt.
66	Z	3688	Mauve–med.
69		3687	Mauve
108		211	Lavender–lt.
104	W	210	Lavender–med.
105		209	Lavender–dk.
110		208	Lavender–vy. dk.
117		3747	Blue Violet–vy. lt.
118		341	Blue Violet–lt.
119		340	Blue Violet–med.
160		813	Blue–lt.
213	▽	369	Pistachio Green–vy. lt.
214		368	Pistachio Green–lt.
216		367	Pistachio Green–dk.
397		453	Shell Gray–lt.
398		452	Shell Gray–med.
399		451	Shell Gray–dk.

Step 2: Backstitch (1 strand)

216		367	Pistachio Green–dk.
403		310	Black

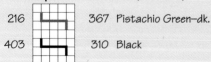

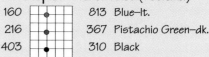

Step 3: French Knot (1 strand)

160		813	Blue–lt.
216		367	Pistachio Green–dk.
403		310	Black

Pillow Finishing

Materials
Finished design
1¼ yds. of lt. green Damask fabric
1¾ yds. of 1½" lt. green Candy Heart ribbon

Directions
Allow ¼" seams.

1. Beginning at one corner of finished design, position and pin ribbon in straight lines ½" from outermost stitching on all sides, forming a square. Fold and miter corners. End ribbon at a corner so mitering hides raw edges.

2. Sew both edges of ribbon all around to complete pillow top.

3. Trim pillow top to within ⅜" of the ribbon.

4. To make pillow ruffle, cut three 4½"-wide strips on the bias from Damask fabric. Sew ends of strips together to make one long strip.

5. Fold long fabric strip in half lengthwise. Sew a gathering stitch along long raw edges. Pull threads to gather.

6. Fit gathered ruffle to right side of pillow top with raw edges together. Adjust gathers evenly. Trim off any excess ruffle and sew raw ends together.

7. Using pillow top as a pattern, cut a matching rectangular piece from Damask fabric for pillow back.

8. Pin pillow top to pillow back with right sides together. Sew all around, leaving an opening for turning. Turn right side out. Stuff pillow. Sew opening closed.

Lucy Locket
Left

I lost her pocket

then found it

But flowers

and ribbons

round it

Loads To Do

Sample Information

The sample was stitched on cream Cashel linen 28 over two threads. The finished design size is 16½" x 7½". The fabric was cut 23" x 14".

Stitch Count: 231 x 105

Other Fabrics	Finished Size
Aida 11	21" x 9½"
Aida 18	12⅞" x 5⅞"
Hardanger 22	10½" x 4¾"

Frame Finishing

Colors used for painting the frame are Green Yellow–lt., Slate Gray, Tan–lt., Yellow–lt., and Rose–pale. Also used was a .25 permanent black lining pen.

Anchor		DMC	
Step 1:		Cross Stitch (2 strands)	
1			White
300		745	Yellow–lt. pale
300		745	Yellow–lt.pale (1 strand)
891		676	Old Gold–lt.
892		225	Shell Pink–vy. lt.

892		225	Shell Pink–vy. lt. (1 strand)
893		224	Shell Pink–lt.
893		224	Shell Pink–lt. (1 strand)
894		223	Shell Pink–med.
896		3721	Shell Pink–dk.
975		3753	Antique Blue–ultra vy. lt.
920		932	Antique Blue–lt.
921		931	Antique Blue–med.
213		369	Pistachio Green–vy. lt.
214		368	Pistachio Green–lt.
214		368	Pistachio Green–lt. (1 strand)
216		367	Pistachio Green–dk.
942		738	Tan–vy. lt.
307		3827	Golden Brown–vy. lt.
363		436	Tan
370		434	Brown–lt.
4146		950	Peach Pecan–dk.
914		3064	Pecan–lt.
936		632	Pecan–dk.
900		3024	Brown Gray–vy. lt.
397		453	Shell Gray–lt.
400		414	Steel Gray–dk.
401		413	Pewter Gray–dk.
403		310	Black

Step 2: Backstitch (1 strand)

896		3721	Shell Pink–dk.
921		931	Antique Blue–med.
216		367	Pistachio Green–dk.
403		310	Black

Step 3: Long Stitch (1 strand)

896		3721	Shell Pink–dk.
216		367	Pistachio Green–dk.
363		436	Tan

Step 4: French Knot (1 strand)

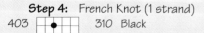

403		310	Black

Step 5: Beads

	02002	Yellow Creme
	00165	Christmas Red
	00168	Sapphire
	00561	Ice Green
	00081	Jet

Loads to Do
Left

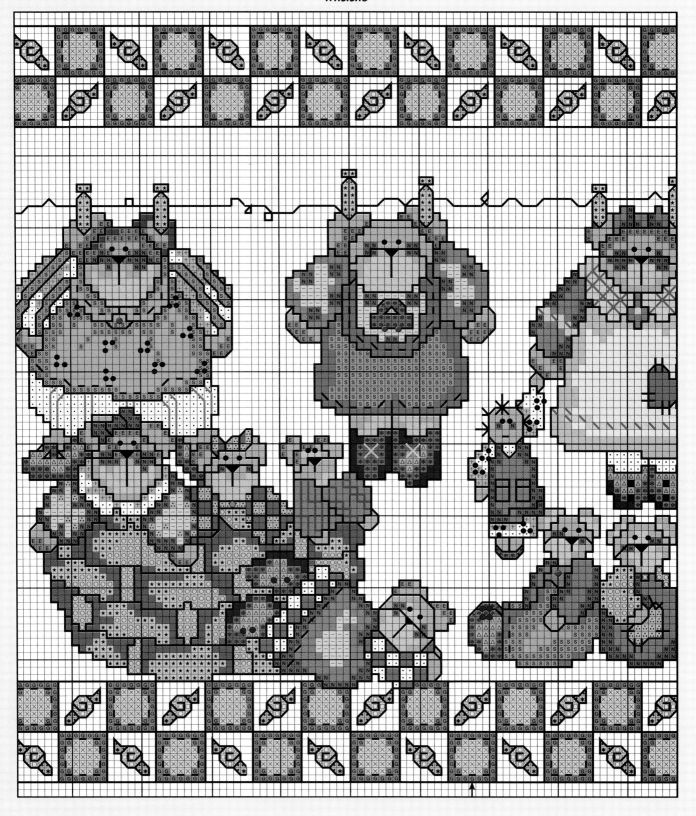

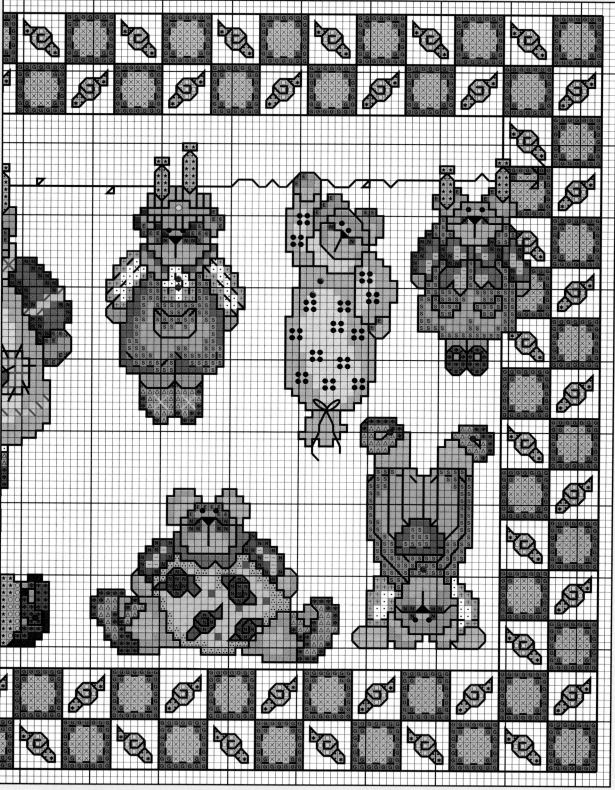

Cherries & Rosebuds

Sample Information
The sample was stitched on periwinkle Pastel linen 28 over two threads. The finished design size is 4⅞" x 11⅞". The fabric was cut 11" x 18".

Stitch Count: 68 x 166

Other Fabrics	Finished Size
Aida 11	6⅛" x 15⅛"
Aida 18	3¾" x 9¼"
Hardanger 22	3⅛" x 7½"

Frame Finishing
Colors used for painting the frame are Beige—vy. lt. and Orange Yellow—lt.

Anchor		DMC	

Step 1: Cross Stitch (2 strands)

292		3078	Golden Yellow—vy. lt.
907	P	3821	Straw
306		3820	Straw—dk.
9	△	760	Salmon
25		3326	Rose—lt.
27	✳	899	Rose—med.

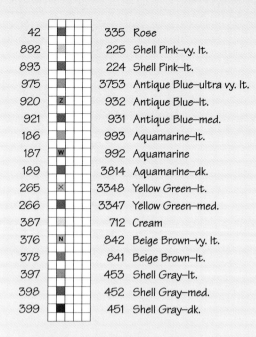

42		335	Rose
892		225	Shell Pink—vy. lt.
893		224	Shell Pink—lt.
975		3753	Antique Blue—ultra vy. lt.
920	Z	932	Antique Blue—lt.
921		931	Antique Blue—med.
186		993	Aquamarine—lt.
187	W	992	Aquamarine
189		3814	Aquamarine—dk.
265	✕	3348	Yellow Green—lt.
266		3347	Yellow Green—med.
387		712	Cream
376	N	842	Beige Brown—vy. lt.
378		841	Beige Brown—lt.
397		453	Shell Gray—lt.
398		452	Shell Gray—med.
399		451	Shell Gray—dk.

Step 2: Backstitch (1 strand)

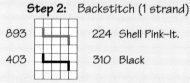

893		224	Shell Pink—lt.
403		310	Black

Step 3: French Knot (1 strand)

403	●	310	Black

Top

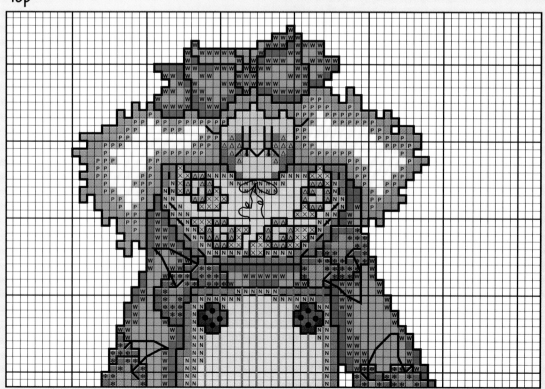

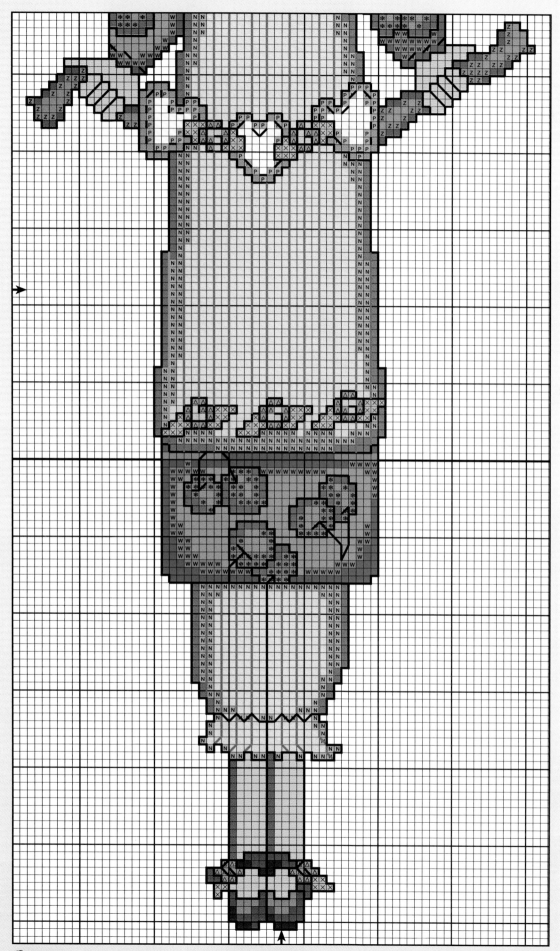

Bottom

Pink Bow

Stitch Count: 50 x 23

Fabrics
Aida 11
Aida 14
Aida 18
Hardanger 22

Finished Size
4½" x 2⅛"
3⅝" x 1⅝"
2¾" x 1¼"
2¼" x 1"

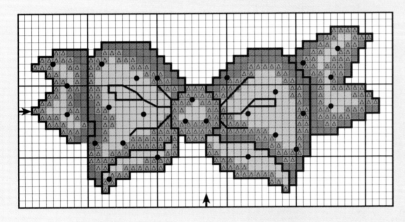

Anchor		DMC	

Step 1: Cross Stitch (2 strands)

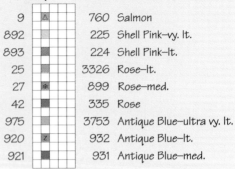

9	△	760	Salmon
892		225	Shell Pink–vy. lt.
893		224	Shell Pink–lt.
25		3326	Rose–lt.
27	✳	899	Rose–med.
42		335	Rose
975		3753	Antique Blue–ultra vy. lt.
920	z	932	Antique Blue–lt.
921		931	Antique Blue–med.

Step 2: Backstitch (1 strand)

403		310	Black

Step 3: Long Stitch (1 strand)

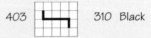

403		310	Black

Hearts

Stitch Count: 35 x 46

Fabrics
Aida 11
Aida 14
Aida 18
Hardanger 22

Finished Size
3⅛" x 4⅛"
2½" x 3¼"
2" x 2½"
1⅝" x 2⅛"

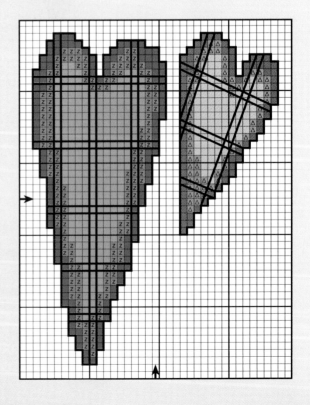

Heart & Hand

Stitch Count: 47 x 40

Fabrics
Aida 11
Aida 14
Aida 18
Hardanger 22

Finished Size
4¼" x 3⅝"
3⅜" x 2⅞"
2⅝" x 2¼"
2⅛" x 1⅞"

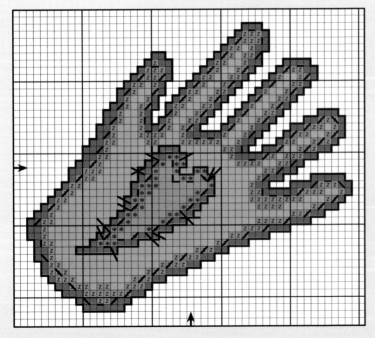

Large Cherries

Stitch Count: 30 x 38

Fabrics	Finished Size
Aida 11	2¾" x 3½"
Aida 14	2⅛" x 2¾"
Aida 18	1⅝" x 2⅛"
Hardanger 22	1⅜" x 1¾"

Anchor		DMC	
Step 1:		Cross Stitch (2 strands)	
25		3326	Rose–lt.
27	✳	899	Rose–med.
42		335	Rose
920		932	Antique Blue–lt.
921		931	Antique Blue–med.
264		772	Pine Green–lt.
265	×	3348	Yellow Green–lt.
266		3347	Yellow Green–med.

Anchor		DMC	
Step 2:		Backstitch (1 strand)	
306		3820	Straw–dk.
403		310	Black

Anchor		DMC	
Step 3:		French Knot (1 strand)	
403	●	310	Black

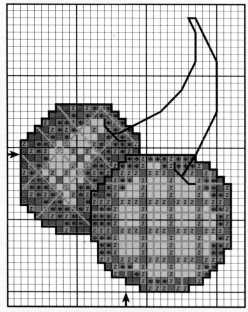

Small Cherries

Stitch Count: 38 x 28

Fabrics	Finished Size
Aida 11	3½" x 2½"
Aida 14	2¾" x 2"
Aida 18	2⅛" x 1½"
Hardanger 22	1¾" x 1¼"

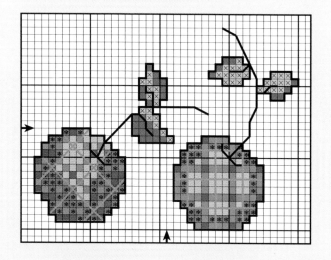

Roses Border

Stitch Count: 73 x 26

Fabrics	Finished Size
Aida 11	6⅝" x 2⅜"
Aida 14	5¼" x 1⅞"
Aida 18	4" x 1½"
Hardanger 22	3⅜" x 1⅛"

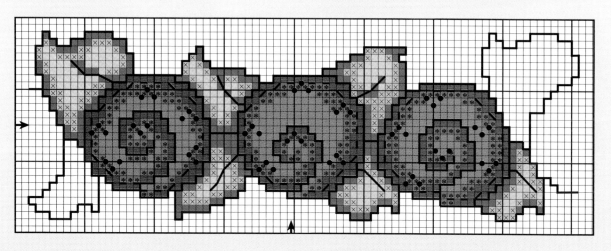

Angel Wings

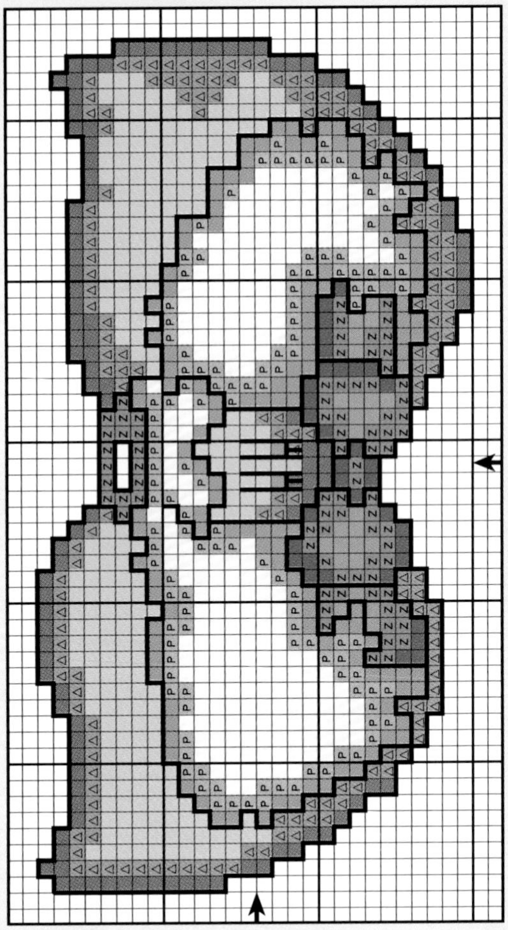

Stitch Count: 53 x 28

Fabrics	Finished Size
Aida 11	4¾" x 2½"
Aida 14	3¾" x 2"
Aida 18	3" x 1½"
Hardanger 22	2⅜" x 1¼"

Anchor		DMC	

Step 1: Cross Stitch (2 strands)

Anchor		DMC	
292		3078	Golden Yellow—vy. lt.
907	P	3821	Straw
306		3820	Straw—dk.
9	△	760	Salmon
892		225	Shell Pink—vy. lt.
893		224	Shell Pink—lt.
975		3753	Antique Blue—ultra vy. lt.
920	Z	932	Antique Blue—lt.
921		931	Antique Blue—med.

Step 2: Backstitch (1 strand)

403		310	Black

Plantin' Time

Stitch Count: 36 x 42

Fabrics	Finished Size
Aida 11	3¼" x 3⅞"
Aida 14	2⅝" x 3"
Aida 18	2" x 2⅜"
Hardanger 22	1⅝" x 1⅞"

Anchor		DMC	

Step 1: Cross Stitch (2 strands)

Anchor		DMC	
8		761	Salmon—lt.
9	N	760	Salmon
11		3328	Salmon—dk.
975		3753	Antique Blue—ultra vy. lt.
920	O	932	Antique Blue—lt.
921		931	Antique Blue—med.
213		369	Pistachio Green—vy. lt.
214	E	368	Pistachio Green—lt.
215		320	Pistachio Green—med.

Step 2: Backstitch (1 strand)

403		310	Black

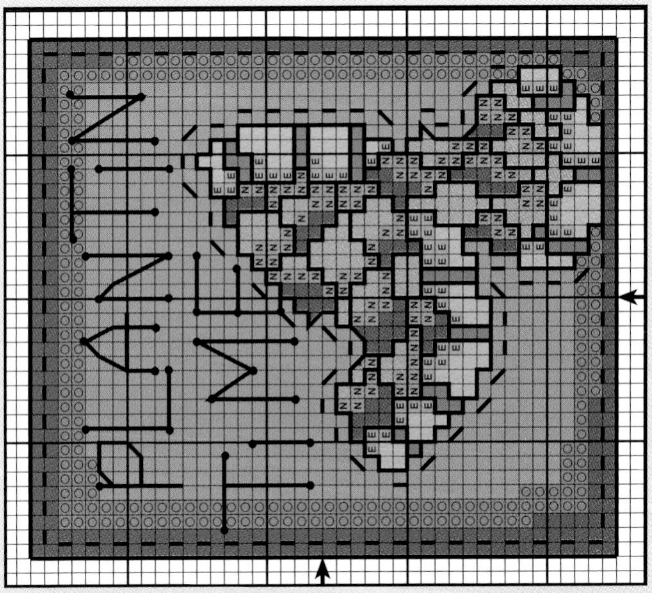

Night-time Barn

Stitch Count: 81 x 27

Fabrics	Finished Size
Aida 11	7⅜" x 2½"
Aida 14	5¾" x 1⅞"
Aida 18	4½" x 1½"
Hardanger 22	3⅝" x 1¼"

Anchor   DMC

Step 1: Cross Stitch (2 strands)

Anchor		DMC	
292		3078	Golden Yellow–vy. lt.
8		761	Salmon–lt.
9	N	760	Salmon
11		3328	Salmon–dk.
928		598	Turquoise–lt.
167	X	597	Turquoise
1039		3810	Turquoise–dk.
213		369	Pistachio Green–vy. lt.
214	E	367	Pistachio Green–lt.
215		320	Pistachio Green–med.
363		436	Tan
309		435	Brown–vy. lt.
900		647	Beaver Gray–med.
8581	✶	646	Beaver Gray–dk.

Step 2: Backstitch (1 strand)

Anchor		DMC	
363		436	Tan
403		310	Black

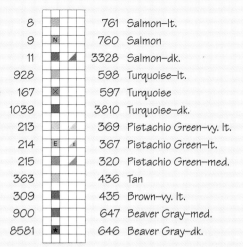

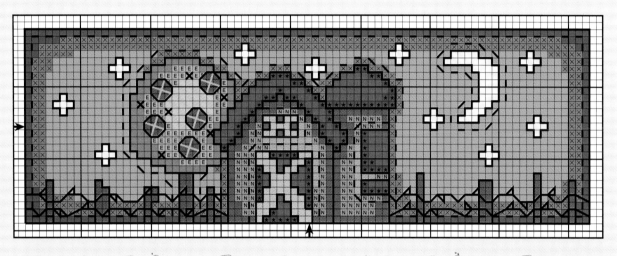

Calico Cat

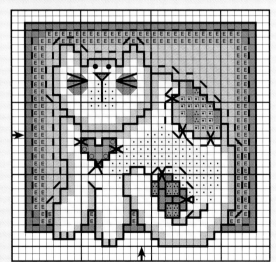

Anchor   DMC

Step 1: Cross Stitch (2 strands)

Anchor		DMC	
386	·	746	Off White
292		3078	Golden Yellow–vy. lt.
907		3822	Straw–lt.
25		3326	Rose–lt.
27		899	Rose–med.
975		3753	Antique Blue–ultra vy. lt.
920	o	932	Antique Blue–lt.
213		369	Pistachio Green–vy. lt.
214	E	368	Pistachio Green–lt.
215		320	Pistachio Green–med.
942	·	738	Tan–vy. lt.
363		436	Tan

Step 2: Backstitch (1 strand)

Anchor		DMC	
403		310	Black

Step 3: French Knot (1 strand)

Anchor		DMC	
403		310	Black

Stitch Count:
33 x 31

Fabrics	Finished Size
Aida 11	3" x 2⅞"
Aida 14	2⅞" x 2¼"
Aida 18	1⅞" x 1¾"
Hardanger 22	1½" x 1⅜"

Quilted Hearts

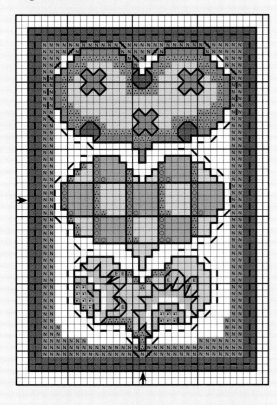

Stitch Count: 35 x 51

Fabrics	Finished Size
Aida 11	3⅛" x 4⅝"
Aida 14	2½" x 3⅝"
Aida 18	2" x 2⅞"
Hardanger 22	1⅝" x 2⅜"

Anchor		DMC	

Step 1: Cross Stitch (2 strands)

Anchor		DMC	
292		3078	Golden Yellow–vy. lt.
907		3822	Straw–lt.
9	N	760	Salmon
11		3328	Salmon–dk.
48		818	Baby Pink
25		3326	Rose–lt.
27		899	Rose–med.
975		3753	Antique Blue–ultra vy. lt.
920	○	932	Antique Blue–lt.
849		927	Slate Green–med.
213		369	Pistachio Green–vy. lt.
214	E	368	Pistachio Green–lt.
942		738	Tan–vy. lt.
363		436	Tan

Step 2: Backstitch (1 strand)

	DMC	
403	310	Black

Overalls

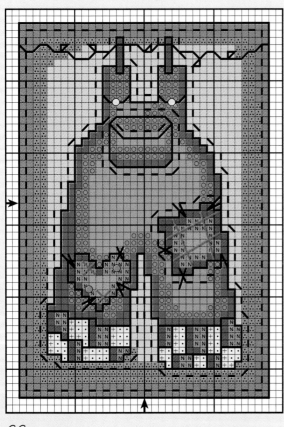

Stitch Count: 36 x 52

Fabrics	Finished Size
Aida 11	3¼" x 4¾"
Aida 14	2⅝" x 3¾"
Aida 18	2" x 2⅞"
Hardanger 22	1⅝" x 2⅜"

Anchor		DMC	

Step 1: Cross Stitch (2 strands)

Anchor		DMC	
386	·	746	Off White
886	+	677	Old Gold–vy. lt.
48		818	Baby Pink
25		3326	Rose–lt.
27		899	Rose–med.
8		761	Salmon–lt.
9	N	760	Salmon
11		3328	Salmon–dk.
975		3753	Antique Blue–ultra vy. lt.
920	○	932	Antique Blue–lt.
921		931	Antique Blue–med.
309		435	Brown–vy. lt.

Step 2: Backstitch (1 strand)

921 | 931 Antique Blue–med.

403 | 310 Black

Step 3: Beads

○ 62041 Frosted Buttercup

● 62049 Frosted Spring Green

Stacked Animals

Stitch Count: 49 x 100

Fabrics	Finished Size
Aida 11	4½" x 9⅛"
Aida 14	3½" x 7⅞"
Aida 18	2¾" x 5½"
Hardanger 22	2¼" x 4½"

Anchor   **DMC**

Step 1: Cross Stitch (2 strands)

Anchor		DMC	
386	·	746	Off White
292		3078	Golden Yellow–vy. lt.
891		676	Old Gold–lt.
8		761	Salmon–lt.
9	N	760	Salmon
11		3328	Salmon–dk.
48		818	Baby Pink
25		3326	Rose–lt.
27		899	Rose–med.
975		3753	Antique Blue–ultra vy. lt.
920	○	932	Antique Blue–lt.
921		931	Antique Blue–med.
942	·	738	Tan–vy. lt.
363		436	Tan
309		435	Brown–vy. lt.
900		647	Beaver Gray–med.
8581	★	646	Beaver Gray–dk.
401		844	Beaver Gray–ultra dk.

Step 2: Backstitch (1 strand)

403 | 310 Black

Step 3: French Knot (1 strand)

403 ● | 310 Black

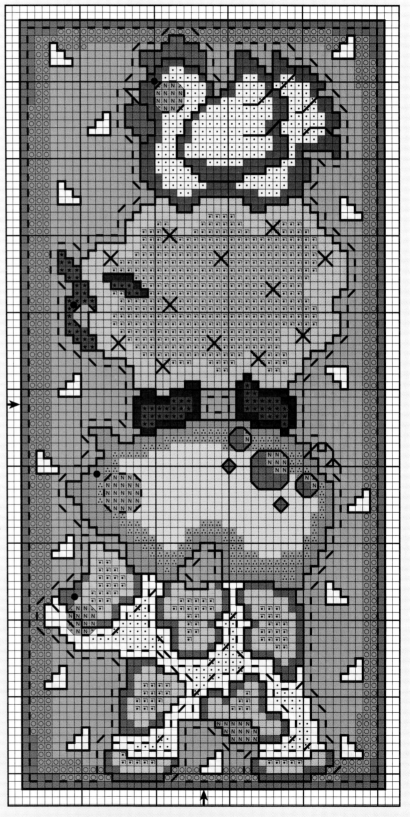

Farm Angels

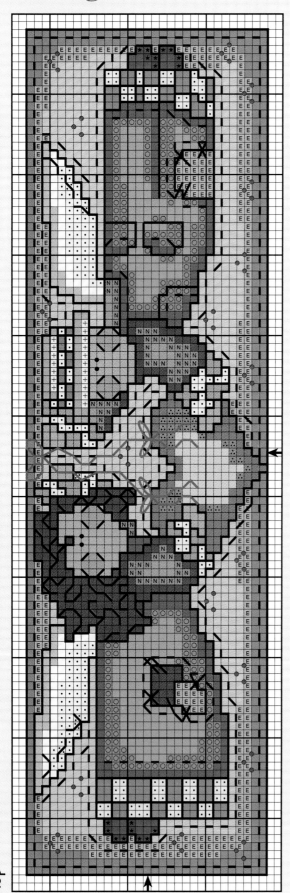

Stitch Count: 105 x 31

Other Fabrics	Finished Size
Aida 11	9½" x 2⅞"
Aida 14	7½" x 2¼"
Aida 18	5⅞" x 1¾"
Hardanger 22	4¾" x 1⅜"

Anchor		DMC	

Step 1: Cross Stitch (2 strands)

Anchor		DMC	
386	·	746	Off White
292		3078	Golden Yellow–vy. lt.
907		3822	Straw–lt.
886	+	677	Old Gold–vy. lt.
891		676	Old Gold–lt.
4146		754	Peach–lt.
48		818	Baby Pink
25	∴	3326	Rose–lt.
27		899	Rose–med.
8		761	Salmon–lt.
9	N	760	Salmon
11		3328	Salmon–dk.
975		3753	Antique Blue–ultra vy. lt.
920	○	932	Antique Blue–lt.
921		931	Antique Blue–med.
849		927	Slate Green–med.
213		369	Pistachio Green–vy. lt.
214	E	368	Pistachio Green–lt.
215		320	Pistachio Green–med.
309		435	Brown–vy. lt.
900		647	Beaver Gray–med.
8581	★	646	Beaver Gray–dk.

Step 2: Backstitch (1 strand)

403		310	Black

Step 3: Long Stitch (1 strand)

403		310	Black

Step 4: French Knot (1 strand)

403	•	310	Black

Step 5: Beads

	•	62004	Frosted Autumn

Farm Boy & Farm Girl

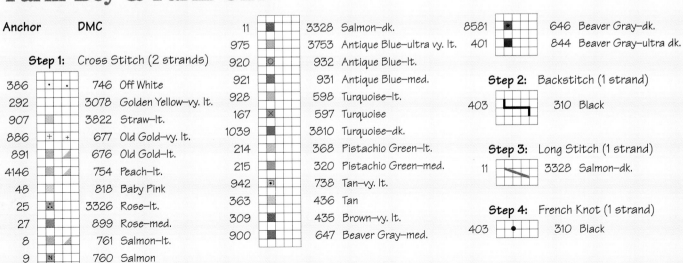

Anchor		DMC	
Step 1:		Cross Stitch (2 strands)	
386		746	Off White
292		3078	Golden Yellow–vy. lt.
907		3822	Straw–lt.
886	+	677	Old Gold–vy. lt.
891		676	Old Gold–lt.
4146		754	Peach–lt.
48		818	Baby Pink
25		3326	Rose–lt.
27		899	Rose–med.
8		761	Salmon–lt.
9	N	760	Salmon

11		3328	Salmon–dk.
975		3753	Antique Blue–ultra vy. lt.
920	O	932	Antique Blue–lt.
921		931	Antique Blue–med.
928		598	Turquoise–lt.
167	×	597	Turquoise
1039		3810	Turquoise–dk.
214		368	Pistachio Green–lt.
215		320	Pistachio Green–med.
942		738	Tan–vy. lt.
363		436	Tan
309		435	Brown–vy. lt.
900		647	Beaver Gray–med.

8581	★	646	Beaver Gray–dk.
401		844	Beaver Gray–ultra dk.
Step 2:		Backstitch (1 strand)	
403		310	Black
Step 3:		Long Stitch (1 strand)	
11		3328	Salmon–dk.
Step 4:		French Knot (1 strand)	
403	●	310	Black

Farm Boy

Sample Information

The sample was stitched on antique white Lugana 25 over two threads. The finished design size is 4¾" x 4⅝". The fabric was cut 11" x 11".

Stitch Count: 59 x 58

Other Fabrics	Finished Size
Aida 11	5⅜" x 5¼"
Aida 14	4¼" x 4⅛"
Aida 18	3¼" x 3¼"
Hardanger 22	2⅝" x 2⅝"

Frame Finishing

Colors used for painting the frame are Orange Yellow–lt. and Tan–lt. Four animal rubber stamps and a .25 permanent black lining pen were also used.

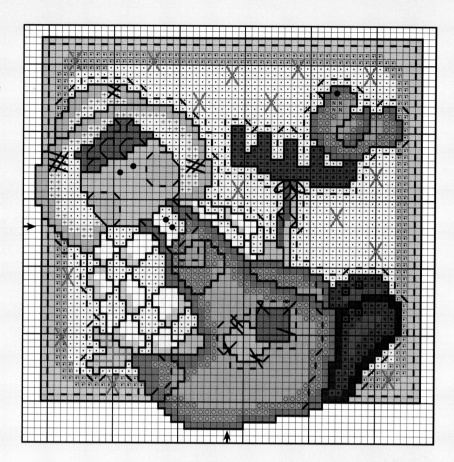

Farm Girl

Sample Information

The sample was stitched on antique white Lugana 25 over two threads. The finished design size is 4¾" x 4⅝". The fabric was cut 11" x 11".

Stitch Count: 59 x 58

Other Fabrics	Finished Size
Aida 11	5⅜" x 5¼"
Aida 14	4¼" x 4⅛"
Aida 18	3¼" x 3¼"
Hardanger 22	2⅝" x 2⅝"

Frame Finishing

Colors used for painting the frame are Pink–lt. and Pink–dk. Four animal rubber stamps and a .25 permanent black lining pen were also used.

Beary Spooky

Sample Information

The sample was stitched on navy Aida 14. The finished design size is 11⅞" x 7½". The fabric was cut 18" x 14".

Stitch Count: 166 x 105

Other Fabrics	Finished Size
Aida 11	15⅛" x 9½"
Aida 18	9¼" x 5⅞"
Hardanger 22	7½" x 4¾"

Anchor		DMC	

Step 1: Cross Stitch (2 strands)

Anchor	symbol	DMC	Color
1	●		White
1	◩		White (1 strand)
921		931	Antique Blue—med. (1 strand)
1			White (1 strand)
	×		
876		3816	Celadon Green (1 strand)
297		743	Yellow—med.
303	W	742	Tangerine—lt.
304	P	741	Tangerine—med.
316		740	Tangerine
330		947	Burnt Orange
66		3688	Mauve—med.
69		3687	Mauve
1019		3803	Mauve—med. dk.
343		3752	Antique Blue—vy. lt.
921		931	Antique Blue—med.
922		930	Antique Blue—dk.
217		3817	Celadon Green—lt.
876		3816	Celadon Green
877	K	3815	Celadon Green—dk.
213		369	Pistachio Green—vy. lt.
214	Z	368	Pistachio Green—lt.
216		367	Pistachio Green—dk.
933		543	Beige Brown—ultra vy. lt.
942		738	Tan—vy. lt.
363	✎	436	Tan
370		434	Brown—lt.
376		842	Beige Brown—vy. lt.
378		841	Beige Brown—lt.
900		3024	Brown Gray—vy. lt.
397		3072	Beaver Gray—vy. lt.
900		648	Beaver Gray—lt.
8581	♥	647	Beaver Gray—med.
905		645	Beaver Gray—vy. dk.
401		413	Pewter Gray—dk.
403		310	Black

Step 2: Backstitch (1 strand)

Anchor		DMC	Color
297		743	Yellow—med.
216		367	Pistachio Green—dk.
			Charcoal Gray mohair floss

Step 3: French Knot (1 strand)

Anchor		DMC	Color
403	●	310	Black

Step 4: Beads

		DMC	Color
	○	02011	Victorian Gold

Frame Finishing

Colors used for painting the frame are Orange and Gray—vy. dk. Also used was a .25 permanent black lining pen.

Beary Spooky

Left

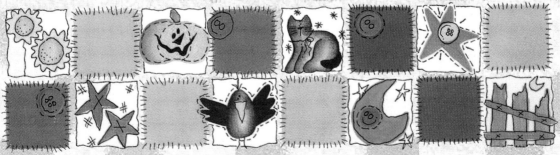

Halloween Placemat

Sample Information

The sample was stitched on prairie sunset Rustico 14. The finished design size for one motif is 1" x ¾". The fabric was cut 13" x 18".

Machine-stitch around design fabric ½" in from raw edges. From the top and left of machine-stitching, count down and in seven squares to begin first motif. Allow six grid squares between motifs.

Stitch Count for one motif: 14 x 11

Other Fabrics	Finished Size
Aida 11	1¼" x 1"
Aida 18	¾" x ⅝"
Hardanger 22	⅝" x ½"

Anchor		DMC	

Step 1: Cross Stitch (2 strands)

Anchor		DMC	
306		725	Topaz
303		742	Tangerine–lt.
316		740	Tangerine
316	z	970	Pumpkin–lt.
330	★	947	Burnt Orange
76		961	Wild Rose–dk.
98		553	Violet–med.
145		334	Baby Blue–med.
239		702	Kelly Green
268		937	Avocado Green–med.
309		435	Brown–vy. lt.
400		414	Steel Gray–dk.
401		413	Pewter Gray–dk.
403	•	310	Black

Step 2: Backstitch (1 strand)

403		310	Black

Step 3: French Knot (1 strand)

403	•	310	Black

Step 4: Lazy Daisy (1 strand)

403		310	Black

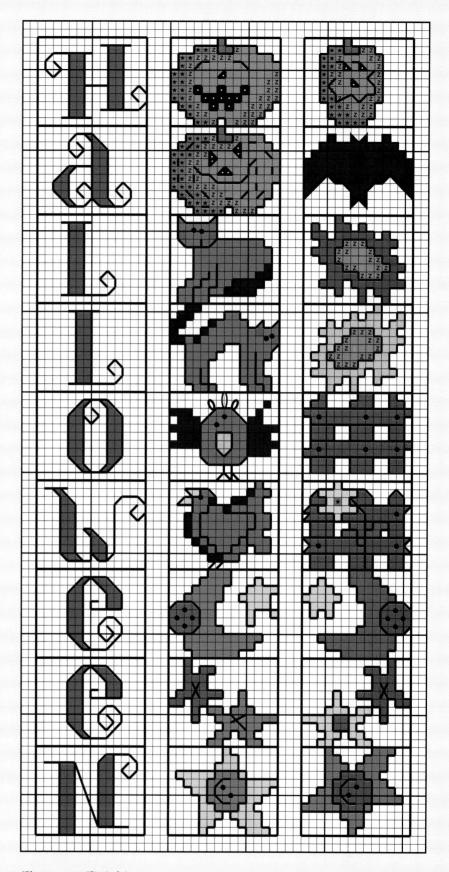

Placemat Finishing

Remove loose warp and weft threads from fabric on all sides to create fringe.

Harvest Patch

Sample Information

The sample was stitched on antique white Cashel linen 28 over two threads. The finished design size is 3⅝" x 3⅝". The fabric was cut 10" x 10".

Stitch Count: 50 x 50

Other Fabrics	Finished Size
Aida 11	4½" x 4½"
Aida 18	2¾" x 2¾"
Hardanger 22	2¼" x 2¼"

Anchor		DMC	

Step 1: Cross Stitch (2 strands)

Anchor		DMC	
386	–	746	Off White
886		677	Old Gold–vy. lt.
891		676	Old Gold–lt.
8		761	Salmon–lt.
10		3712	Salmon–med.
13		347	Salmon–vy. dk.
158		775	Baby Blue–vy. lt.
159	K	3325	Baby Blue–lt.
154		3755	Baby Blue
978		322	Navy Blue–vy. lt.
214	×	368	Pistachio Green–lt.
215		320	Pistachio Green–med.
942		738	Tan–vy. lt.
363	★	436	Tan
309		435	Brown–vy. lt.

Step 2: Backstitch (1 strand)

Anchor	DMC	
10	3712	Salmon–med.
13	347	Salmon–vy. dk.
154	3755	Baby Blue
215	320	Pistachio Green–med.
398	415	Pearl Gray
403	310	Black

Step 3: Long Stitch (1 strand)

Anchor	DMC	
891	676	Old Gold–lt.

Step 4: French Knot (1 strand)

Anchor	DMC	
403	310	Black

Frame Finishing

Colors used for painting the frame are Rose–med., Slate Blue, Off White, Gold, and Green–dk.

Melon Bear

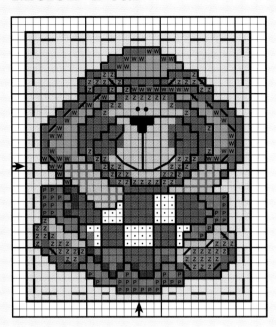

Other Fabrics

Fabric	Finished Size
Aida 11	2¾" x 3⅛"
Aida 18	1⅝" x 2"
Hardanger 22	1⅜" x 1⅝"

Anchor		DMC	

Step 1: Cross Stitch (2 strands)

Anchor		DMC	
893		224	Shell Pink–lt.
894		223	Shell Pink–med.
896		3721	Shell Pink–dk.
159		3325	Baby Blue–lt.
145	W	334	Baby Blue–med.
978		322	Navy Blue–vy. lt.
266		471	Avocado Green–vy. lt.
268	P	937	Avocado Green–med.
387		712	Cream
942		738	Tan–vy. lt.
363	Z	436	Tan
309		435	Brown–vy. lt.

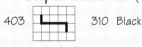

Step 2: Backstitch (1 strand)

Anchor		DMC	
403		310	Black

Step 3: French Knot (1 strand)

Anchor		DMC	
403	●	310	Black

Sample Information

The sample was centered and stitched on a purchased baby bib with a white Aida 14 inset. The finished design size is 2⅛" x 2½".

Stitch Count: 30 x 35

Love Banner

Stitch Count: 25 x 37

Fabrics	Finished Size
Aida 11	2¼" x 3⅜"
Aida 14	1¾" x 2⅝"
Aida 18	1⅜" x 2"
Hardanger 22	1⅛" x 1⅝"

Anchor		DMC	

Step 1: Cross Stitch (2 strands)

Anchor		DMC	
886		677	Old Gold–vy. lt.
891		676	Old Gold–lt.
8		761	Salmon–lt.
10		3712	Salmon–med.
978		322	Navy Blue–vy. lt.
363	★	436	Tan

Step 2: Backstitch (1 strand)

Anchor		DMC	
13		347	Salmon–vy. dk.
371		433	Brown–med.
403		310	Black

Step 3: French Knot (1 strand)

Anchor		DMC	
371	●	433	Brown–med.

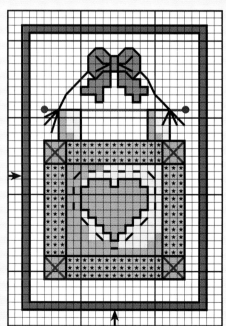

Apple Basket

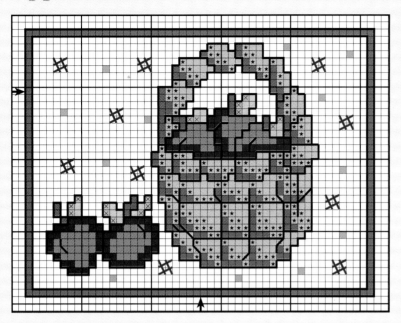

Stitch Count: 50 x 37

Fabrics	Finished Size
Aida 11	4½" x 3⅜"
Aida 14	3⅝" x 2⅝"
Aida 18	2¾" x 2"
Hardanger 22	2¼" x 1⅝"

Anchor		DMC	

Step 1: Cross Stitch (2 strands)

Anchor		DMC	
10		3712	Salmon–med.
13		347	Salmon–vy. dk.
154		3755	Baby Blue
978		322	Navy Blue–vy. lt.
213		369	Pistachio Green–vy. lt.
214	×	368	Pistachio Green–lt.
942		738	Tan–vy. lt.
363	★	436	Tan
309		435	Brown–vy. lt.

Step 2: Backstitch (1 strand)

13		347	Salmon–vy. dk.
403		310	Black

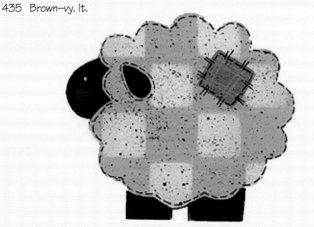

Kitty Kat

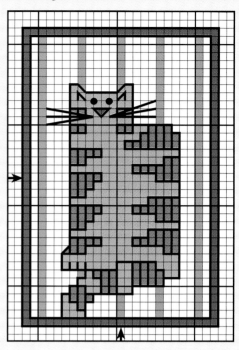

Stitch Count: 25 x 37

Fabrics	Finished Size
Aida 11	2¼" x 3⅜"
Aida 14	1¾" x 2⅝"
Aida 18	1⅜" x 2"
Hardanger 22	1⅛" x 1⅝"

Step 1: Cross Stitch (2 strands)

Anchor		DMC	
891		676	Old Gold–lt.
8		761	Salmon–lt.
10		3712	Salmon–med.
154		3755	Baby Blue
978		322	Navy Blue–vy. lt.
309		435	Brown–vy. lt.

Step 2: Backstitch (1 strand)

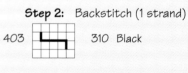

403		310	Black

Step 3: Long Stitch (1 strand)

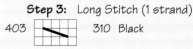

403		310	Black

Step 4: French Knot (1 strand)

403		310	Black

Bombear Jacket

Sample Information

The sample was stitched on antique white Cashel linen 28 over two threads. The finished design size is 3⅝" x 2⅞". The fabric was cut 10" x 9".

Stitch Count: 50 x 40

Other Fabrics	Finished Size
Aida 11	4½" x 3⅝"
Aida 18	2¾" x 2¼"
Hardanger 22	2¼" x 1⅞"

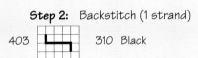

Anchor		DMC	
Step 1:	Cross Stitch (2 strands)		
8		761	Salmon—lt.
10		3712	Salmon—med.
13		347	Salmon—vy. dk.
978		322	Navy Blue—vy. lt.
213		369	Pistachio Green—vy. lt.
214		368	Pistachio Green—lt.
215		320	Pistachio Green—med.
942		738	Tan—vy. lt.
363		436	Tan
309		435	Brown—vy. lt.
Step 2:	Backstitch (1 strand)		
403		310	Black
Step 3:	French Knot (1 strand)		
403		310	Black

Jacket Finishing

Cut linen to within ½" all around stitching for an edging. Using an iron, press ½" edging to wrong side of stitching, keeping edges straight and taking bulk from corners. Use fray preventer to avoid fraying on corners.

Using pressed stitching as a pattern, cut a piece of fusible webbing. Apply fusible webbing to wrong side of stitching following manufacturer's instructions. Place stitching on right front top of purchased jacket. Press to fuse.

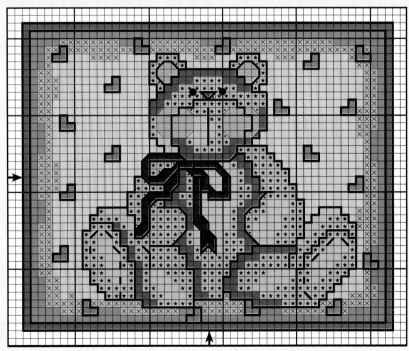

Pumpkins

Stitch Count: 62 x 34

Fabrics	Finished Size
Aida 11	5⅝" x 3⅛"
Aida 14	4½" x 2⅜"
Aida 18	3½" x 1⅞"
Hardanger 22	2⅞" x 1½"

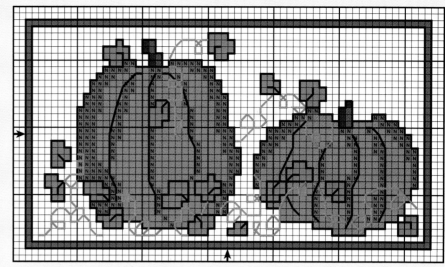

Anchor   DMC

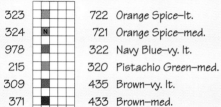

Step 1:   Cross Stitch (2 strands)

Anchor		DMC	
323		722	Orange Spice–lt.
324	N	721	Orange Spice–med.
978		322	Navy Blue–vy. lt.
215		320	Pistachio Green–med.
309		435	Brown–vy. lt.
371		433	Brown–med.

Step 2:   Backstitch (1 strand)

215		320	Pistachio Green–med.
403		310	Black

Sunflower Bouquet

Stitch Count: 49 x 55

Fabrics	Finished Size
Aida 11	4½" x 5"
Aida 14	3½" x 3⅞"
Aida 18	2¾" x 3"
Hardanger 22	2¼" x 2½"

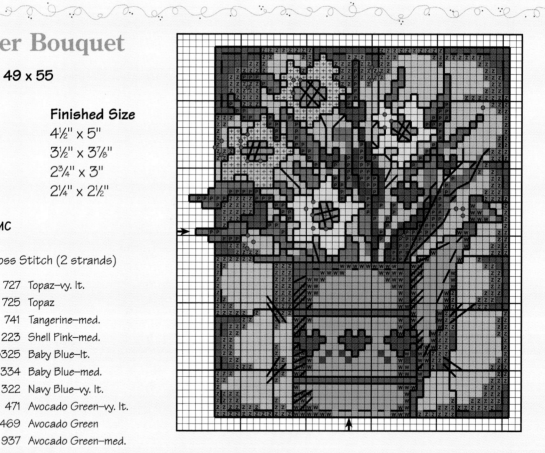

Anchor   DMC

Step 1:   Cross Stitch (2 strands)

Anchor		DMC	
293		727	Topaz–vy. lt.
306	+	725	Topaz
304	▽	741	Tangerine–med.
894		223	Shell Pink–med.
159		3325	Baby Blue–lt.
145	W	334	Baby Blue–med.
978		322	Navy Blue–vy. lt.
266		471	Avocado Green–vy. lt.
267		469	Avocado Green
268	P	937	Avocado Green–med.
942		738	Tan–vy. lt.
363	Z	436	Tan
309		435	Brown–vy. lt.

Step 2:   Backstitch (1 strand)

403		310	Black

Step 3:   Long Stitch (1 strand)

403		310	Black

Step 4:   French Knot (1 strand)

894	●	223	Shell Pink–med.

Schoolhouse

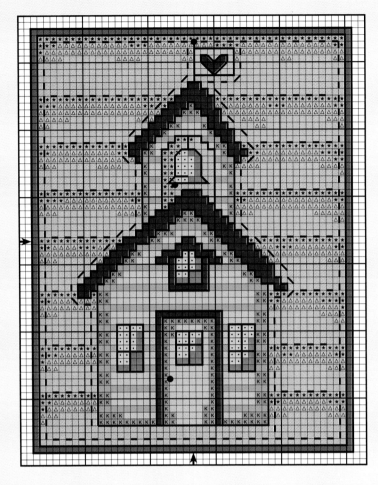

Fabrics	Finished Size
Aida 11	4½" x 5¾"
Aida 14	3½" x 4½"
Aida 18	2¾" x 3½"
Hardanger 22	2¼" x 2⅞"

Anchor		DMC	

Step 1: Cross Stitch (2 strands)

13		347	Salmon–vy. dk.
158		775	Baby Blue–vy. lt.
159	K	3325	Baby Blue–lt.
154		3755	Baby Blue
978		322	Navy Blue–vy. lt.
942		738	Tan–vy. lt.
362	△	437	Tan–lt.
363	★	436	Tan
397		762	Pearl Gray–vy. lt.
398		415	Pearl Gray

Step 2: Backstitch (1 strand)

403		310	Black

Step 3: French Knot (1 strand)

403	●	310	Black

Cottage Window

Stitch Count: 31 x 47

Fabrics	Finished Size
Aida 11	2⅞" x 4¼"
Aida 14	2¼" x 3⅜"
Aida 18	1¾" x 2⅝"
Hardanger 22	1⅜" x 2⅛"

Anchor		DMC	

Step 1: Cross Stitch (2 strands)

386	–	746	Off White
907		3822	Straw–lt.
10		3712	Salmon–med.
154		3755	Baby Blue
978		322	Navy Blue–vy. lt.
214	✕	368	Pistachio Green–lt.

Step 2: Backstitch (1 strand)

403		310	Black

Step 3: French Knot (1 strand)

154	●	3755	Baby Blue

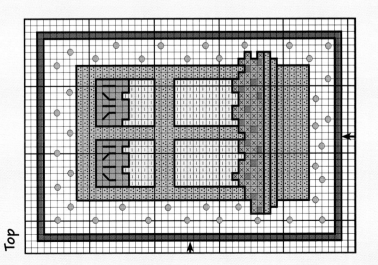

Scarecrow

Sample Information

The sample was stitched on oatmeal Floba 25 over two threads. The finished design size is 4⁷⁄₈" x 10⁵⁄₈". The fabric was cut 11" x 17".

Stitch Count: 61 x 133

Other Fabrics	Finished Size
Aida 11	5½" x 12⅛"
Aida 14	4⅜" x 9½"
Aida 18	3⅜" x 7⅜"
Hardanger 22	2¾" x 6"

Anchor		DMC	

Step 1: Cross Stitch (2 strands)

Anchor		DMC	
293		727	Topaz–vy. lt.
306	+	725	Topaz
303		742	Tangerine–lt.
304	▽	741	Tangerine–med.
316		970	Pumpkin–lt.
10		3712	Salmon–med.
13		347	Salmon–vy. dk.
893		224	Shell Pink–lt.
894		223	Shell Pink–med.
896		3721	Shell Pink–dk.
159		3325	Baby Blue–lt.
145	W	334	Baby Blue–med.
266		471	Avocado Green–vy. lt.
267		469	Avocado Green
268	P	937	Avocado Green–med.
942		738	Tan–vy. lt.
363	z	436	Tan
309		435	Brown–vy. lt.
8581		647	Beaver Gray–med.

905	♠	646	Beaver Gray–dk.
401		844	Beaver Gray–ultra dk.

Step 2: Backstitch (1 strand)

267		469	Avocado Green
403		310	Black

Step 3: French Knot (1 strand)

403	●	310	Black

Frame Finishing

Colors used for painting the frame are Beige–lt., Red–vy. dk., Gray–vy. dk., Slate Gray, Slate Blue, Tan–lt., and Tan. Also used were a 5 x 5 stencil, a .25 permanent black lining pen, and fruit-wood liquid wood stain.

Top

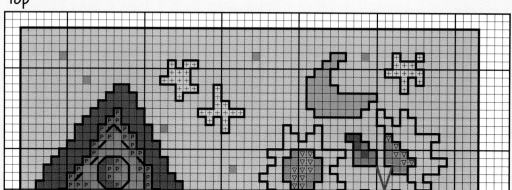

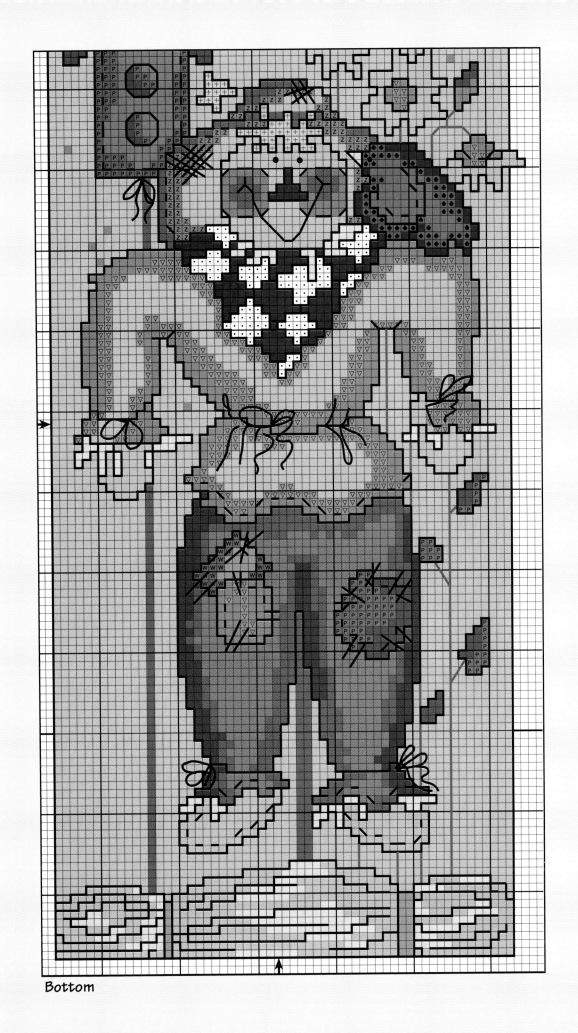

Bottom

Harvest Wheelbarrow

Stitch Count: 81 x 42

Fabrics

Fabrics	Finished Size
Aida 11	7⅜" x 3⅞"
Aida 14	5¾" x 3"
Aida 18	4½" x 2⅜"
Hardanger 22	3⅝" x 1⅞"

Anchor	DMC

Step 1: Cross Stitch (2 strands)

Anchor		DMC	
306	+	725	Topaz
303		742	Tangerine–lt.
304	▽	741	Tangerine–med.
316		970	Pumpkin–lt.
893		224	Shell Pink–lt.
894		223	Shell Pink–med.
896		3721	Shell Pink–dk.
13		347	Salmon–vy. dk.
266		471	Avocado Green–vy. lt.
267		469	Avocado Green
268	P	937	Avocado Green–med.
387		712	Cream
942		738	Tan–vy. lt.
363	Z	436	Tan
309		435	Brown–vy. lt.
8581		647	Beaver Gray–med.
905	◢	646	Beaver Gray–dk.
401		844	Beaver Gray–ultra dk.

Step 2: Backstitch (1 strand)

Anchor		DMC	
306		725	Topaz
267		469	Avocado Green
403		310	Black

Step 3: Long Stitch (1 strand)

Anchor		DMC	
403		310	Black

Step 4: French Knot (1 strand)

Anchor		DMC	
316	•	970	Pumpkin–lt.

Step 5: Lazy Daisy (1 strand)

Anchor		DMC	
403	⬭	310	Black

Top

Potted Sunflowers

Stitch Count: 82 x 32

Fabrics / Finished Size

Fabrics	Finished Size
Aida 11	7½" x 3"
Aida 14	5⅞" x 2¼"
Aida 18	4½" x 1¾"
Hardanger 22	3¾" x 1½"

Anchor   DMC

Step 1: Cross Stitch (2 strands)

Anchor		DMC	
293		727	Topaz–vy. lt.
306	+	725	Topaz
303		742	Tangerine–lt.
304	▽	741	Tangerine–med.
316		970	Pumpkin–lt.
1047		3825	Pumpkin–pale
324		922	Copper–lt.
266		471	Avocado Green–vy. lt.
267		469	Avocado Green
268	P	937	Avocado Green–med.
387		712	Cream
309		435	Brown–vy. lt.

Step 2: Backstitch (1 strand)

Anchor		DMC	
403	⌐	310	Black

Step 3: Long Stitch (1 strand)

Anchor		DMC	
267	╱	469	Avocado Green
403	╲	310	Black

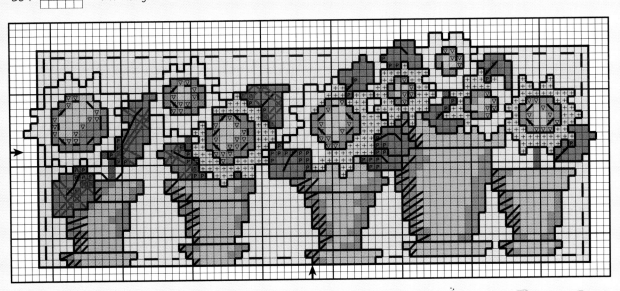

Warm Heart

Stitch Count: 27 x 38

Fabrics / Finished Size

Fabrics	Finished Size
Aida 11	2½" x 3½"
Aida 14	1⅞" x 2¾"
Aida 18	1½" x 2⅛"
Hardanger 22	1¼" x 1¾"

Anchor   DMC

Step 1: Cross Stitch (2 strands)

Anchor		DMC	
386	○	746	Off White
886		677	Old Gold–vy. lt.
891		676	Old Gold–lt.
271		3713	Salmon–vy. lt.
25		3326	Rose–lt.
27	✕	899	Rose–med.
154		3755	Baby Blue

Step 2: Backstitch (1 strand)

Anchor		DMC	
214		368	Pistachio Green–lt.
403	⌐	310	Black

Step 3: French Knot (1 strand)

Anchor		DMC	
819	●	676	Old Gold–lt.

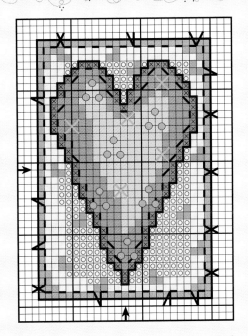

Blue Country

Sample Information

The sample was stitched on daffodil Pastel linen 28 over two threads. The finished design size is 5¾" x 12⅛". The fabric was cut 12" x 19".

Stitch Count: 80 x 170

Other Fabrics	Finished Size
Aida 11	7¼" x 15½"
Aida 18	4½" x 9½"
Hardanger 22	3⅝" x 7¾"

Frame Finishing

Colors used for painting the frame are Beige–vy. lt. and Slate Gray.

Anchor		DMC	
9		760	Salmon
27		899	Rose–med.
42	W	335	Rose
59		326	Rose–vy. dk.
892		225	Shell Pink–vy. lt.
893		224	Shell Pink–lt.
343		3752	Antique Blue–vy. lt.
920	P	932	Antique Blue–lt.
921		931	Antique Blue–med.
387		712	Cream
376	·	842	Beige Brown–vy. lt.
378		841	Beige Brown–lt.
379		840	Beige Brown–med.
397		453	Shell Gray–lt.
398		452	Shell Gray–med.
399		451	Shell Gray–dk.

Step 1: Cross Stitch (2 strands)

Anchor		DMC	
292		3078	Golden Yellow–vy. lt.
907	+	3822	Straw–lt.
306		3820	Straw–dk.

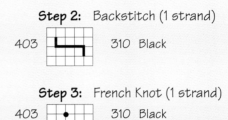

Step 2: Backstitch (1 strand)

403		310	Black

Step 3: French Knot (1 strand)

403	●	310	Black

Top

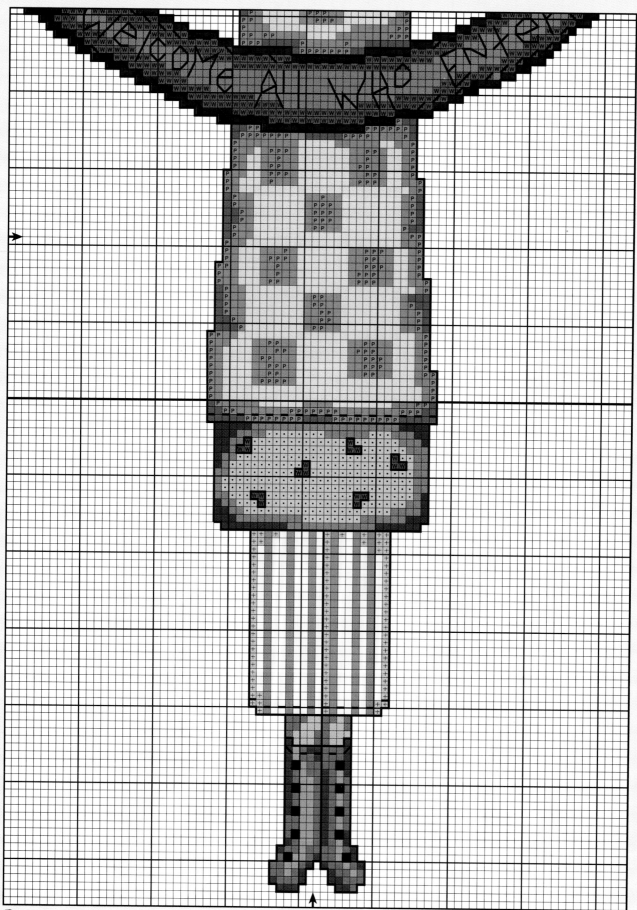

Bottom

Country Hearts

Stitch Count: 19 x 57

Fabrics	Finished Size
Aida 11	1¾" x 5⅛"
Aida 14	1⅜" x 4⅛"
Aida 18	1" x 3⅛"
Hardanger 22	⅞" x 2⅝"

Anchor		DMC	
Step 1:		Cross Stitch (2 strands)	
292		3078	Golden Yellow–vy. lt.
907	+	3822	Straw–lt.
306		3820	Straw–dk.
27		899	Rose–med.
42	W	335	Rose
896		3721	Shell Pink–dk.

Anchor		DMC	
Step 2:		Backstitch (1 strand)	
403		310	Black

Anchor		DMC	
Step 3:		French Knot (1 strand)	
403	●	310	Black

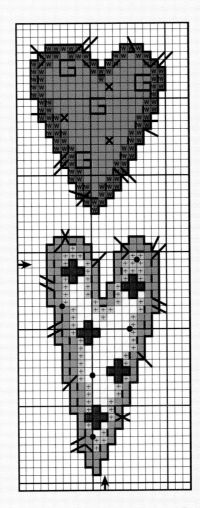

Potted Hearts

Stitch Count: 27 x 52

Fabrics	Finished Size
Aida 11	2½" x 4¾"
Aida 14	1⅞" x 3¾"
Aida 18	1½" x 2⅞"
Hardanger 22	1¼" x 2⅜"

Anchor		DMC	
920	P	932	Antique Blue–lt.
921		931	Antique Blue–med.
266		3347	Yellow Green–med.

Anchor		DMC	
Step 2:		Backstitch (1 strand)	
403		310	Black

Anchor		DMC	
Step 3:		French Knot (1 strand)	
403	●	310	Black

Anchor		DMC	
Step 1:		Cross Stitch (2 strands)	
292		3078	Golden Yellow–vy. lt.
907	+	3822	Straw–lt.
306		3820	Straw–dk.
1047		3825	Pumpkin–pale
323	z	722	Orange Spice–lt.
324		922	Copper–lt.
27		899	Rose–med.
42	W	335	Rose
59		326	Rose–vy. dk.
343		3752	Antique Blue–vy. lt.

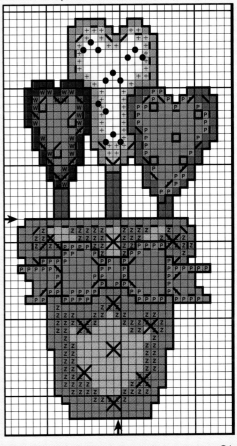

91

Plaid Angel

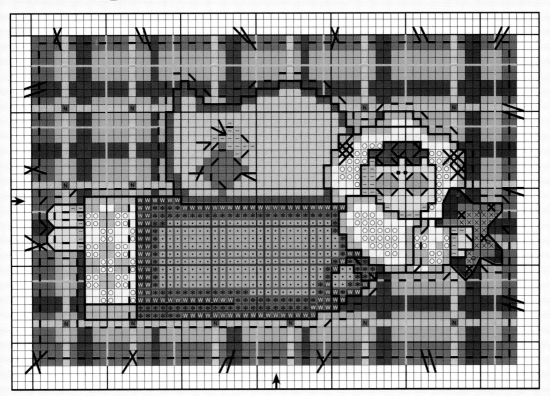

Sample Information

The sample was stitched on white Lugana 25 over two threads. The finished design size is 5⅜" x 3⅝". The fabric was cut 12" x 10".

Stitch Count: 67 x 45

Other Fabrics	Finished Size
Aida 11	6⅛" x 4⅛"
Aida 14	4¾" x 3¼"
Aida 18	3¾" x 2½"
Hardanger 22	3" x 2"

Frame Finishing

Colors used for painting the frame are Red–vy. dk., Beige–lt., Rose–lt., and Rose–med. Also used was a .25 permanent black lining pen.

Step 1: Cross Stitch (2 strands)

Anchor		DMC	
386	○	746	Off White
886		677	Old Gold–vy. lt.
891		676	Old Gold–lt.
8	—	761	Salmon–lt.
9		760	Salmon
271		3713	Salmon–vy. lt.
27	✕	899	Rose–med.
42		335	Rose
59		326	Rose–vy. dk.

Anchor		DMC	
154	·	3755	Baby Blue
154	·	3755	Baby Blue (1 strand)
978	✳	322	Navy Blue–vy. lt.
978		322	Navy Blue–vy. lt. (1 strand)
147	W	312	Navy Blue–lt.
147		312	Navy Blue–lt. (1 strand)
942		738	Tan–vy. lt.
363		436	Tan
309	N	435	Brown–vy. lt. (1 strand)
370		434	Brown–lt.

Step 2: Backstitch (1 strand)

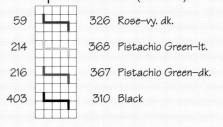

59		326	Rose–vy. dk.
214		368	Pistachio Green–lt.
216		367	Pistachio Green–dk.
403		310	Black

Step 3: Long Stitch (1 strand)

403		310	Black

Step 4: French Knot (1 strand)

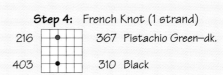

216	●	367	Pistachio Green–dk.
403	●	310	Black

Sitting Chicken

Stitch Count: 29 x 58

Fabrics	Finished Size
Aida 11	2⅝" x 5¼"
Aida 14	2⅛" x 4⅛"
Aida 18	1⅝" x 3¼"
Hardanger 22	1⅜" x 2⅝"

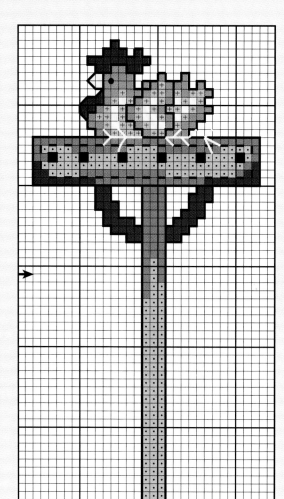

Tote Bag Finishing
Photo on page 92.

Motifs below and on opposite page are stitched on an Aida 14 tote bag. Motifs are stacked with Sitting Chicken (without the post) on top and Baa Baa Black Sheep below it, Pig Patches below the sheep, and How Now Brown Cow on the bottom. Combined motifs are centered on front of tote bag.

Anchor		DMC	

Step 1: Cross Stitch (2 strands)

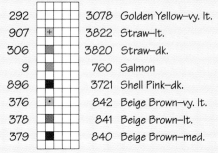

292		3078	Golden Yellow–vy. lt.
907	+	3822	Straw–lt.
306		3820	Straw–dk.
9		760	Salmon
896		3721	Shell Pink–dk.
376	·	842	Beige Brown–vy. lt.
378		841	Beige Brown–lt.
379		840	Beige Brown–med.

Step 2: Backstitch (1 strand)

| 292 | | 3078 | Golden Yellow–vy. lt. |
| 403 | | 310 | Black |

Step 3: French Knot (1 strand)

| 403 | • | 310 | Black |

Pig Patches

Stitch Count: 38 x 25

Fabrics	Finished Size
Aida 11	3½" x 2⅜"
Aida 14	2¾" x 1⅞"
Aida 18	2⅛" x 1½"
Hardanger 22	1¾" x 1⅛"

Anchor		DMC	

Step 1: Cross Stitch (2 strands)

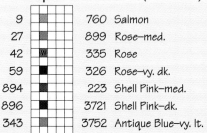

9		760	Salmon
27		899	Rose–med.
42	W	335	Rose
59		326	Rose–vy. dk.
894		223	Shell Pink–med.
896		3721	Shell Pink–dk.
343		3752	Antique Blue–vy. lt.

| 920 | P | 932 | Antique Blue–lt. |

Step 2: Backstitch (1 strand)

| 403 | | 310 | Black |

Step 3: French Knot (1 strand)

| 403 | • | 310 | Black |

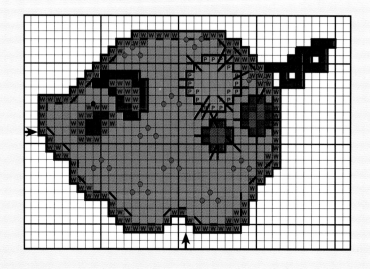

94

How Now Brown Cow

Stitch Count: 39 x 33

Fabrics	Finished Size
Aida 11	3½" x 3"
Aida 14	2¾" x 2⅜"
Aida 18	2⅛" x 1⅞"
Hardanger 22	1¾" x 1½"

Anchor		DMC	
Step 1:	Cross Stitch (2 strands)		
292		3078	Golden Yellow–vy. lt.
907		3822	Straw–lt.
27		899	Rose–med.
42	W	335	Rose
343		3752	Antique Blue–vy. lt.
920	P	932	Antique Blue–lt.
387		712	Cream
942	△	738	Tan–vy. lt.
363		436	Tan
370		434	Brown–lt.
Step 2:	Backstitch (1 strand)		
403		310	Black
Step 3:	French Knot (1 strand)		
403		310	Black

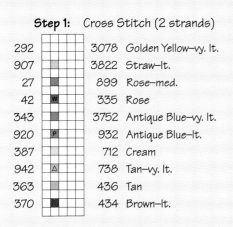

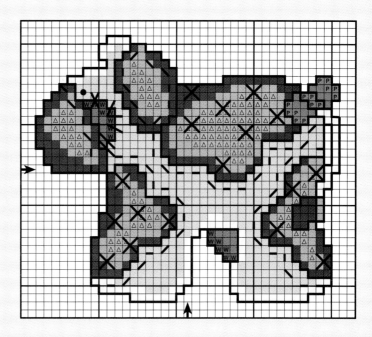

Baa Baa Black Sheep

Stitch Count: 31 x 23

Fabrics	Finished Size
Aida 11	2⅞" x 2⅛"
Aida 14	2¼" x 1⅝"
Aida 18	1¾" x 1¼"
Hardanger 22	1⅜" x 1"

Anchor		DMC	
Step 1:	Cross Stitch (2 strands)		
9		760	Salmon
27		899	Rose–med.
397		453	Shell Gray–lt.
398		452	Shell Gray–med.
399		451	Shell Gray–dk.
Step 2:	Backstitch (1 strand)		
403		310	Black
Step 3:	French Knot (1 strand)		
403		310	Black

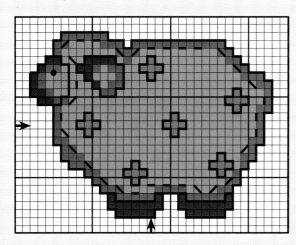

Handmade Treasures

Sample Information
The sample was stitched on wedgewood Murano 30 over two threads. The finished design size is 12⅛" x 14⅜". The fabric was cut 19" x 21".

Stitch Count: 182 x 216

Other Fabrics	Finished Size
Aida 11	16½" x 19⅝"
Aida 14	13" x 15⅜"
Aida 18	10⅛" x 12"
Hardanger 22	8¼" x 9⅞"

Frame Finishing
Colors used for painting the frame are Tan–lt., Rose–pale, Rose–dk., Green Yellow–lt., Green–dk., Yellow–med., and Gold. Also used was a .25 permanent black lining pen.

Top Left

Bottom Left

Bottom Middle

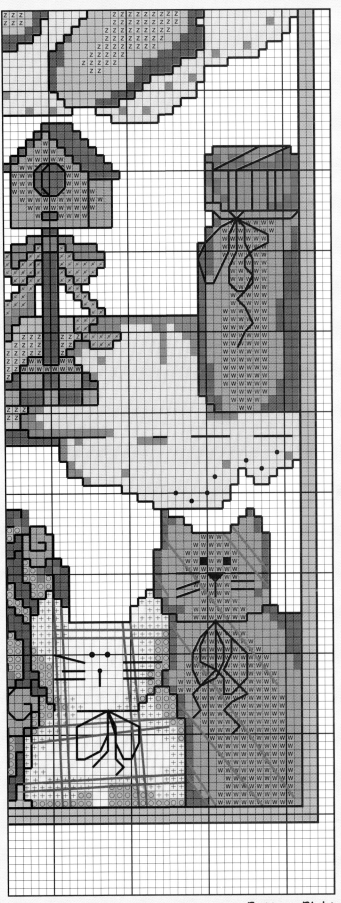

Bottom Right

Anchor		DMC	

Step 1: Cross Stitch (2 strands)

Anchor		DMC	
386		746	Off White
886	+	677	Old Gold–vy. lt.
891	O	676	Old Gold–lt.
4146		754	Peach–lt.
8	W	761	Salmon–lt.
9		760	Salmon
11	◣	3328	Salmon–dk.
975	✗	3753	Antique Blue–ultra vy. lt.
920		932	Antique Blue–lt.
921	▽	931	Antique Blue–med.
922		930	Antique Blue–dk.
928		598	Turquoise–lt.
167		597	Turquoise
1039	◣	3810	Turquoise–dk.
213		369	Pistachio Green–vy. lt.
214	P	368	Pistachio Green–lt.
215		320	Pistachio Green–med.
387		712	Cream
942	Z	738	Tan–vy. lt.
363		436	Tan
309		435	Brown–vy. lt.
900		3024	Brown Gray–vy. lt.
1040		3023	Brown Gray–lt.
8581		3022	Brown Gray–med.

Step 2: Backstitch (1 strand)

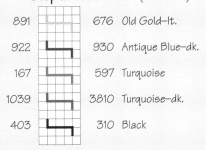

Anchor	DMC	
891	676	Old Gold–lt.
922	930	Antique Blue–dk.
167	597	Turquoise
1039	3810	Turquoise–dk.
403	310	Black

Step 3: French Knot (1 strand)

Anchor		DMC	
403	●	310	Black

Winter

Sing a song of winter
of frosty clouds in air!
sing a song
of
snowflakes
falling
everywhere

Song Of Winter

Sample Information

The sample was stitched on amaretto Murano 30 over two threads. The finished design size is 8⅜" x 6½". The fabric was cut 15" x 13".

Stitch Count: 125 x 98

Other Fabrics	Finished Size
Aida 11	11⅜" x 8⅞"
Aida 14	8⅞" x 7"
Aida 18	7" x 5⅛"
Hardanger 22	5⅝" x 4½"

Frame Finishing

Colors used for painting the frame are Green Yellow–lt., Yellow–med., and Gold.

Anchor		DMC	

Step 1: Cross Stitch (2 strands)

Anchor		DMC	
387		712	Cream
891		676	Old Gold–lt.
890		729	Old Gold–med.
326		720	Orange Spice–dk.
8		761	Salmon–lt.
897		221	Shell Pink–vy. dk.
921		931	Antique Blue–med.
861		3363	Pine Green–med.
879		500	Blue Green–vy. dk.
388		3033	Mocha Brown–vy. lt.
899		3782	Mocha Brown–lt.
308		3826	Golden Brown
355		975	Golden Brown–dk.
236		3799	Pewter Gray–vy. dk.

Step 2: Backstitch (1 strand)

Anchor		DMC	
387		712	Cream
890		729	Old Gold–med. (2 strands)
861		3363	Pine Green–med.
403		310	Black

Step 3: French Knot (1 strand)

Anchor		DMC	
403		310	Black

Left

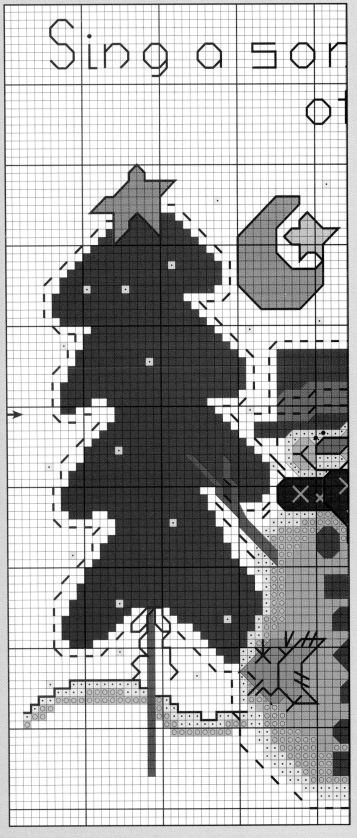

Funky Snowman

Sample Information

The sample was stitched on white Lugana 25 over two threads. The finished design size is 4½" x 5". The fabric was cut 11" x 11".

Stitch Count: 57 x 62

Other Fabrics	Finished Size
Aida 11	5⅛" x 5⅝"
Aida 14	4⅛" x 4½"
Aida 18	3⅛" x 3½"
Hardanger 22	2⅝" x 2⅞"

Frame Finishing

Colors used for painting the frame are Brown–dk. and Brown–lt. A mitten rubber stamp was also used.

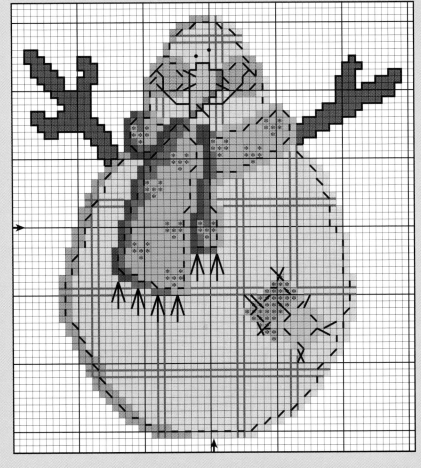

Anchor		DMC	
Step 1:		Cross Stitch (2 strands)	
328		3341	Apricot
11		351	Coral
9		760	Salmon
968	*	778	Antique Mauve–vy. lt.
154		3755	Baby Blue
978		322	Navy Blue–vy. lt.
147		312	Navy Blue–lt.
214		368	Pistachio Green–lt.
3877		822	Beige Gray–lt.
376		842	Beige Brown–vy. lt.
378		841	Beige Brown–lt.
379		840	Beige Brown–med.

Anchor		DMC	
Step 2:		Backstitch (1 strand)	
379		840	Beige Brown–med.
403		310	Black

Anchor		DMC	
Step 3:		French Knot (1 strand)	
403	•	310	Black

Mittens

Stitch Count: 65 x 44

Fabrics	Finished Size
Aida 11	5⅞" x 4"
Aida 14	4⅝" x 3⅛"
Aida 18	3⅝" x 2½"
Hardanger 22	3" x 2"

Anchor   **DMC**

Step 1: Cross Stitch (2 strands)

Anchor		DMC	
891		676	Old Gold–lt.
969		316	Antique Mauve–med.
970		315	Antique Mauve–vy. dk.
72		902	Garnet–vy. dk.
154		3755	Baby Blue
376		842	Beige Brown–vy. lt.

Step 2: Backstitch (1 strand)

403		310	Black

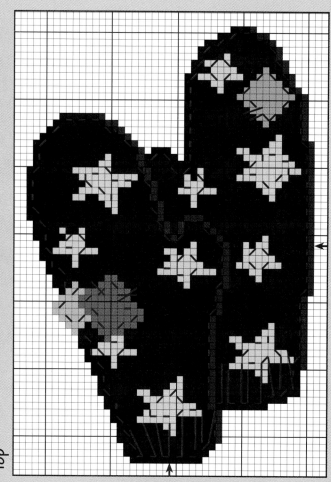

Stitched Stocking

Stitch Count: 37 x 56

Fabrics	Finished Size
Aida 11	3⅜" x 5⅛"
Aida 14	2⅝" x 4"
Aida 18	2" x 3⅛"
Hardanger 22	1⅝" x 2½"

Anchor   **DMC**

Step 1: Cross Stitch (2 strands)

Anchor		DMC	
891		676	Old Gold–lt.
969		316	Antique Mauve–med.
970		315	Antique Mauve–vy. dk.
978		322	Navy Blue–vy. lt.
928		598	Turquoise–lt.
167		597	Turquoise
1039		3810	Turquoise–dk.
214		368	Pistachio Green–lt.
942		738	Tan–vy. lt.
363		436	Tan

Step 2: Backstitch (1 strand)

403		310	Black

Step 3: Long Stitch (1 strand)

403		310	Black

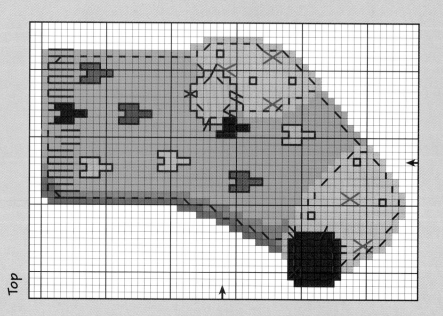

Snow Friend

Stitch Count: 45 x 57

Fabrics

Fabrics	Finished Size
Aida 11	4⅛" x 5⅛"
Aida 14	3¼" x 4"
Aida 18	2½" x 3⅛"
Hardanger 22	2" x 2½"

Anchor		DMC	

Step 1: Cross Stitch (2 strands)

386		746	Off White
886		677	Old Gold–vy. lt.
891		676	Old Gold–lt.
328		3341	Apricot
11		351	Coral
271		3713	Salmon–vy. lt.
8		761	Salmon–lt.
9		760	Salmon
970		315	Antique Mauve–vy. dk.
154		3755	Baby Blue
978		322	Navy Blue–vy. lt.
379		840	Beige Brown–med.
403		310	Black

Step 2: Backstitch (1 strand)

214		368	Pistachio Green–lt. (2 strands)
403		310	Black

Step 3: Long Stitch (1 strand)

403		310	Black

Step 4: French Knot (1 strand)

403		310	Black

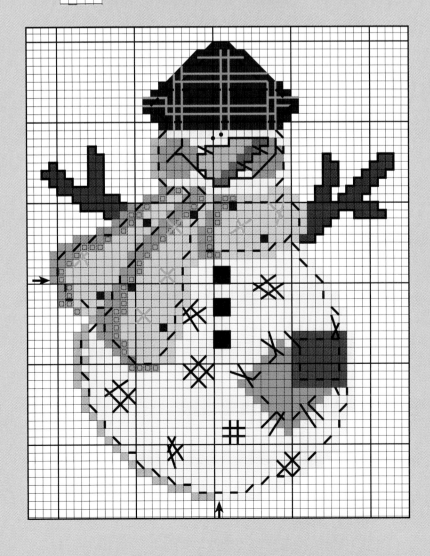

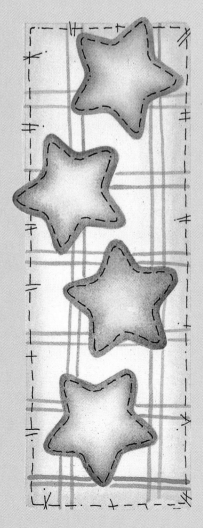

107

Christmas Is More

Sample Information

The sample was stitched on platinum Cashel linen 28 over two threads. The finished design size is 14¼" x 9¾". The fabric was cut 21" x 16".

Stitch Count: 200 x 137

Other Fabrics	Finished Size
Aida 11	18⅛" x 12½"
Aida 18	11⅛" x 7⅝"
Hardanger 22	9⅛" x 6¼"

Frame Finishing

Colors used for painting the frame are Slate Gray and Slate Blue.

Anchor		DMC	
Step 1:		Cross Stitch (2 strands)	
387	· ·	712	Cream
386		746	Off White
292	– –	3078	Golden Yellow–vy. lt.
886		677	Old Gold–vy. lt.
891		676	Old Gold–lt.
907	✕	3822	Straw–lt.

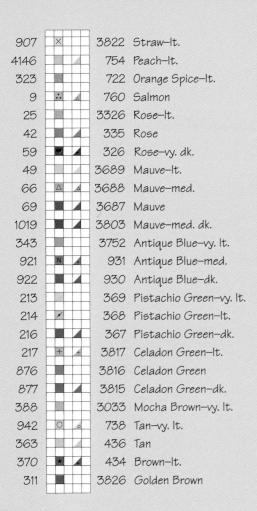

907		3822	Straw–lt.
4146		754	Peach–lt.
323		722	Orange Spice–lt.
9		760	Salmon
25		3326	Rose–lt.
42		335	Rose
59		326	Rose–vy. dk.
49		3689	Mauve–lt.
66		3688	Mauve–med.
69		3687	Mauve
1019		3803	Mauve–med. dk.
343		3752	Antique Blue–vy. lt.
921		931	Antique Blue–med.
922		930	Antique Blue–dk.
213		369	Pistachio Green–vy. lt.
214		368	Pistachio Green–lt.
216		367	Pistachio Green–dk.
217		3817	Celadon Green–lt.
876		3816	Celadon Green
877		3815	Celadon Green–dk.
388		3033	Mocha Brown–vy. lt.
942		738	Tan–vy. lt.
363		436	Tan
370		434	Brown–lt.
311		3826	Golden Brown

Step 2: Backstitch (1 strand)

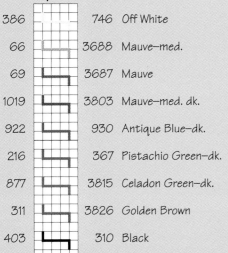

386		746	Off White
66		3688	Mauve–med.
69		3687	Mauve
1019		3803	Mauve–med. dk.
922		930	Antique Blue–dk.
216		367	Pistachio Green–dk.
877		3815	Celadon Green–dk.
311		3826	Golden Brown
403		310	Black

Step 3: French Knot (1 strand)

386		746	Off White
891		676	Old Gold–lt.
59		326	Rose–vy. dk.
922		930	Antique Blue–dk.
217		3817	Celadon Green–lt.
877		3815	Celadon Green–dk.
403		310	Black

Top Left

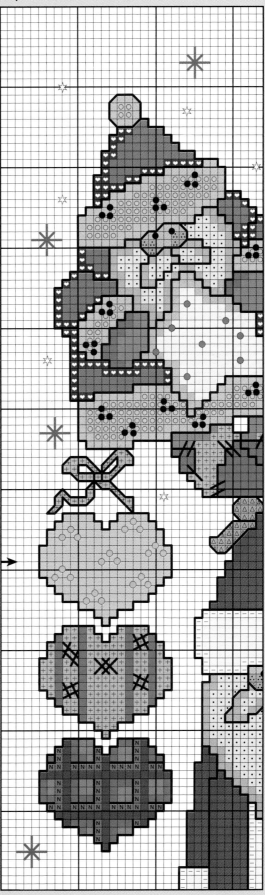

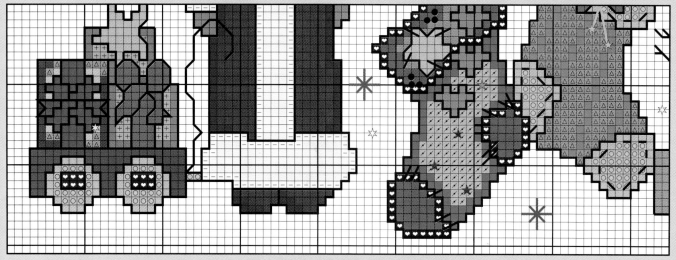

Bottom Left

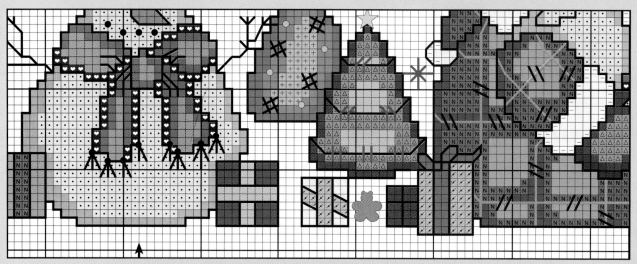

Bottom Middle

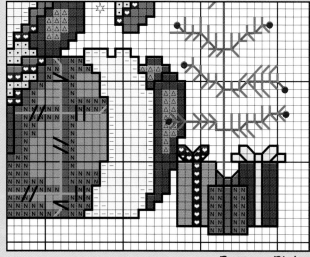

Bottom Right

Step 4: Embellishments

☆	Gold Straw Star with bead 62031 Frosted Gold
★	Green Star Sequins with bead 62031 Frosted Gold
★	Red Star Sequins with bead 62031 Frosted Gold
★	Purple Star Sequins with bead 62031 Frosted Gold
★	Blue Star Sequins with bead 62031 Frosted Gold
★	Gold Star Charm
⬤	12120 Glass Treasures Teddy Bear
✩	12061 Glass Treasures White Star
✩	12108 Glass Treasures Crystal Star Tree Top

Angel In My Pocket

Sample Information

The sample was stitched on sand Belfast linen 32 over two threads. The finished design size is 6⅛" x 8½". The fabric was cut 13" x 15".

Stitch Count: 98 x 135

Other Fabrics	Finished Size
Aida 11	8⅞" x 12¼"
Aida 14	7" x 9⅝"
Aida 18	5⅛" x 7½"
Hardanger 22	4½" x 6⅛"

Anchor		DMC	

Step 1: Cross Stitch (2 strands)

Anchor		DMC	
891		676	Old Gold–lt.
890	z / z	729	Old Gold–med.
4146		754	Peach–lt.
337		3778	Terra Cotta
897		221	Shell Pink–vy. dk.
872		3740	Antique Violet–dk.
878		501	Blue Green–dk.
903		3032	Mocha Brown–med.

Step 2: Backstitch (1 strand)

403		310	Black

Step 3: French Knot (1 strand)

403	•	310	Black

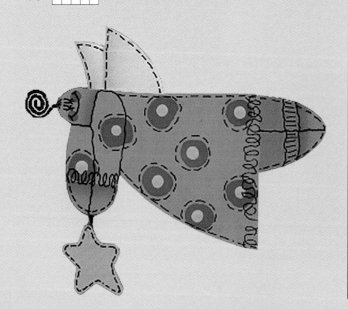

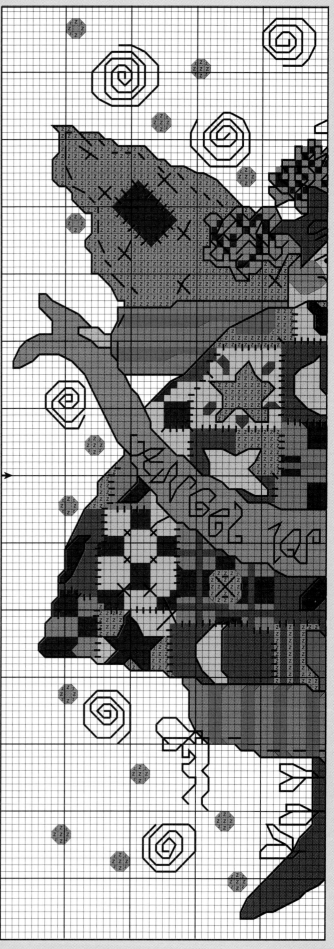

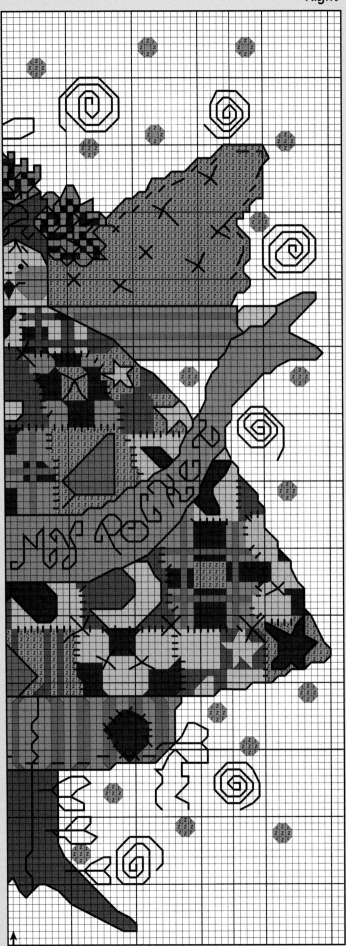

Catch A Falling Star

Stitch Count: 73 x 106

Fabrics	Finished Size
Aida 11	6⅝" x 9⅝"
Aida 14	5¼" x 7⅝"
Aida 18	4" x 5⅞"
Hardanger 22	3⅜" x 4⅞"

Anchor		DMC	

Step 1: Cross Stitch (2 strands)

Anchor		DMC	
891		676	Old Gold–lt.
890	Z	729	Old Gold–med.
4146		754	Peach–lt.
26	P	3708	Melon–lt.
337		3778	Terra Cotta
897		221	Shell Pink–vy. dk.
872		3740	Antique Violet–dk.
878		501	Blue Green–dk.
903		3032	Mocha Brown–med.

Step 2: Backstitch (1 strand)

Anchor		DMC	
897		221	Shell Pink–vy. dk.
403		310	Black

Step 3: French Knot (1 strand)

Anchor		DMC	
403	•	310	Black

Catch A Falling Star

Hanging From A Star

Stitch Count: 53 x 106

Fabrics | Finished Size

Fabrics	Finished Size
Aida 11	4¾" x 9⅝"
Aida 14	3¾" x 7⅝"
Aida 18	3" x 5⅞"
Hardanger 22	2⅜" x 4⅞"

Anchor		DMC	

Step 1: Cross Stitch (2 strands)

891		676	Old Gold–lt.
890	Z	729	Old Gold–med.
4146		754	Peach–lt.
26	P	3708	Melon–lt.
337		3778	Terra Cotta
897		221	Shell Pink–vy. dk.
872		3740	Antique Violet–dk.
878		501	Blue Green–dk.
903		3032	Mocha Brown–med.

Step 2: Backstitch (1 strand)

403		310	Black

Step 3: French Knot (1 strand)

897	•	221	Shell Pink–vy. dk.
403	•	310	Black

Garland of Stars

Sample Information

The sample was stitched on cream Pastel linen 28 over two threads. The finished design size is 7⅛" x 3¾". The fabric was cut 14" x 10".

Stitch Count: 100 x 52

Other Fabrics	Finished Size
Aida 11	9⅛" x 4¾"
Aida 18	5½" x 2⅞"
Hardanger 22	4½" x 2⅜"

Anchor		DMC	
Step 1:		Cross Stitch (2 strands)	
891		676	Old Gold–lt.
890	Z	729	Old Gold–med.
4146		754	Peach–lt.
26	P	3708	Melon–lt.
337		3778	Terra Cotta
897		221	Shell Pink–vy. dk.
968		778	Antique Mauve–vy. lt.
969		316	Antique Mauve–med.
872		3740	Antique Violet–dk.
878		501	Blue Green–dk.
903		3032	Mocha Brown–med.

Anchor		DMC	
Step 2:	Backstitch (1 strand)		
403		310	Black
Step 3:	French Knot (1 strand)		
897	●	221	Shell Pink–vy. dk.
403	●	310	Black

Garland of Stars

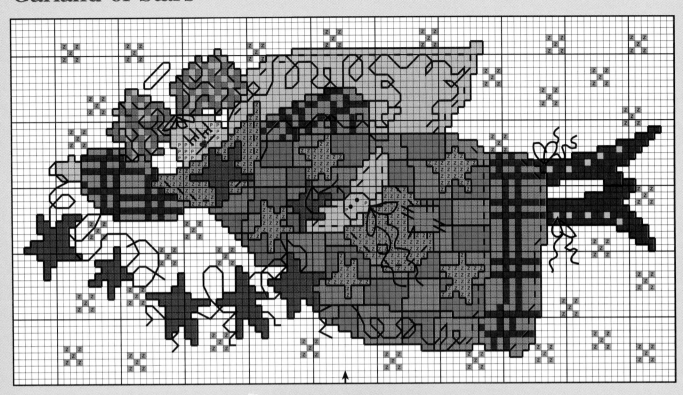

Blessed Star

Fabrics

Aida 11
Aida 14
Aida 18
Hardanger 22

Finished Size

5½" x 4½"
4⅜" x 3⅝"
3⅜" x 2¾"
2¾" x 2¼"

Anchor		DMC	
Step 1:		Cross Stitch (2 strands)	
891		676	Old Gold–lt.
890	Z	729	Old Gold–med.
4146		754	Peach–lt.
26	P	3708	Melon–lt.
872		3740	Antique Violet–dk.
878		501	Blue Green–dk.
879		500	Blue Green–vy. dk.
903		3032	Mocha Brown–med.

	Step 2:		Backstitch (1 strand)	
403			310	Black

	Step 3:		French Knot (1 strand)	
897		•	221	Shell Pink–vy. dk.

Stitch Count: 61 x 50

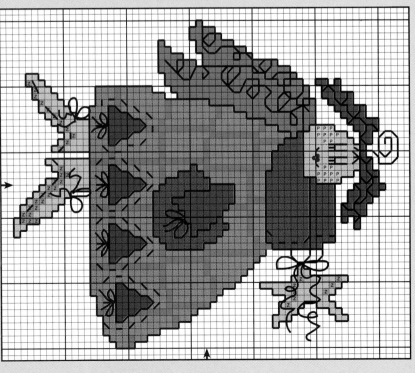

Twinkle Star

Stitch Count: 79 x 40

Fabrics	Finished Size
Aida 11	7⅛" x 3⅝"
Aida 14	5⅝" x 2⅞"
Aida 18	4¾" x 2¼"
Hardanger 22	3⅝" x 1⅞"

Anchor   DMC

Step 1: Cross Stitch (2 strands)

891		676	Old Gold–lt.
890	Z	729	Old Gold–med.
4146		754	Peach–lt.
26	P	3708	Melon–lt.
337		3778	Terra Cotta
897		221	Shell Pink–vy. dk.
872		3740	Antique Violet–dk.

Step 2: Backstitch (1 strand)

891		676	Old Gold–lt.
403		310	Black

Step 3: French Knot (1 strand)

897	•	221	Shell Pink–vy. dk.
403	•	310	Black

Stocking Stuffer

Stitch Count: 61 x 106

Fabrics	Finished Size
Aida 11	5½" x 9⅝"
Aida 14	4⅜" x 7⅝"
Aida 18	3⅜" x 5⅞"
Hardanger 22	2¾" x 4⅞"

Anchor   DMC

Step 1: Cross Stitch (2 strands)

891		676	Old Gold–lt.
890	Z	729	Old Gold–med.
4146		754	Peach–lt.
26	P	3708	Melon–lt.
337		3778	Terra Cotta
897		221	Shell Pink–vy. dk.
872		3740	Antique Violet–dk.
878		501	Blue Green–dk.
903		3032	Mocha Brown–med.

Step 2: Backstitch (1 strand)

337		3778	Terra Cotta
403		310	Black

Step 3: French Knot (1 strand)

403	•	310	Black

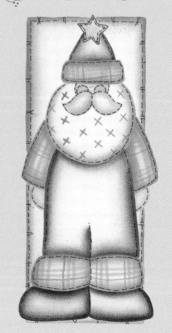

Stocking Stuffer

Warmth & Wooliness

Sample Information
The sample was stitched on mushroom Brittany 28 over two threads. The finished design size is 4⅞" x 6⅜". The fabric was cut 11" x 13".

Stitch Count: 69 x 89

Other Fabrics	Finished Size
Aida 11	6¼" x 8⅛"
Aida 18	3⅞" x 5"
Hardanger 22	3⅛" x 4"

Frame Finishing
Colors used for painting the frame are Green Yellow–lt., Yellow–lt., Aqua–lt., Aqua–med., Brown–med., Rose–lt., and Rose–med. Also used was a .25 permanent black lining pen.

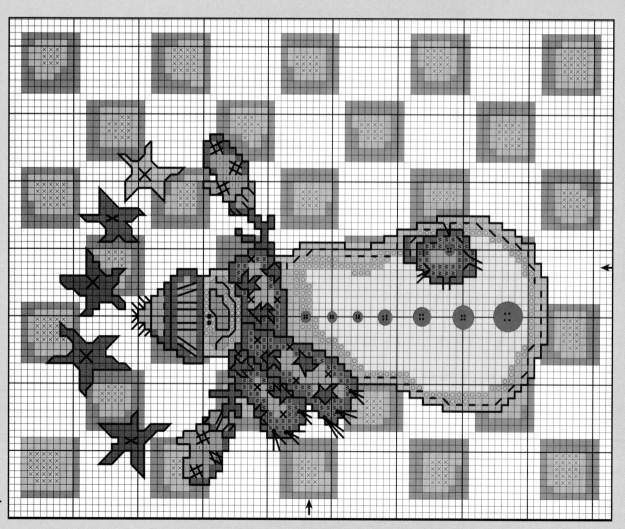

Top

Step 1: Cross Stitch (2 strands)

Anchor		DMC	
304		741	Tangerine–med.
8		761	Salmon–lt.
9		760	Salmon
11		3328	Salmon–dk.
928		598	Turquoise–lt.
167	W	597	Turquoise
1039		3810	Turquoise–dk.
213	×	369	Pistachio Green–vy. lt.

Anchor		DMC	
214		368	Pistachio Green–lt.
215		320	Pistachio Green–med.
885		739	Tan–ultra vy. lt.
942	o	738	Tan–vy. lt.
363		436	Tan
309		435	Brown–vy. lt.

Step 2: Backstitch (1 strand)

403		310	Black

Step 3: French Knot (1 strand)

403	•	310	Black

Step 4: Buttons

	Red
	Green

Cardinal

Stitch Count: 42 x 34

Fabrics	Finished Size
Aida 11	3⅞" x 3⅛"
Aida 14	3" x 2⅜"
Aida 18	2⅜" x 1⅞"
Hardanger 22	1⅞" x 1½"

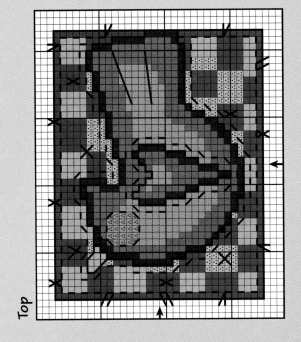

Top

Gingerbread Man

Stitch Count: 50 x 49

Fabrics	Finished Size
Aida 11	4½" x 4½"
Aida 14	3⅝" x 3½"
Aida 18	2¾" x 2¾"
Hardanger 22	2¼" x 2¼"

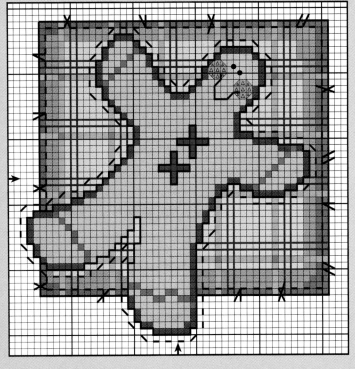

Step 1: Cross Stitch (2 strands)

Anchor		DMC	
891		676	Old Gold–lt.
271		3713	Salmon–vy. lt.
9		760	Salmon
25		3326	Rose–lt.
42	△	335	Rose
59		326	Rose–vy. dk.

Anchor		DMC	
213		369	Pistachio Green–vy. lt
214		368	Pistachio Green–lt.
215		320	Pistachio Green–med
216		367	Pistachio Green–dk.
942		738	Tan–vy. lt.
363		436	Tan
370		434	Brown–lt.

Step 2: Backstitch (1 strand)

59		326	Rose–vy. dk.
403		310	Black

Winter Fire

Anchor DMC

Stitch Count:	Fabrics	Finished Size
47 x 36	Aida 11	4¼" x 3¼"
	Aida 14	3⅜" x 2⅝"
	Aida 18	2⅝" x 2"
	Hardanger 22	2⅛" x 1⅝"

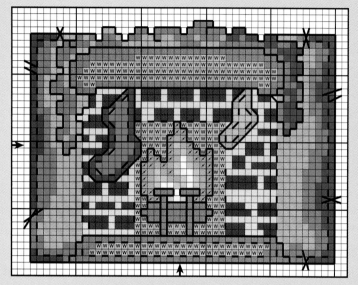

Step 1: Cross Stitch (2 strands)

Anchor		DMC	
292		3078	Golden Yellow–vy. lt.
907		3822	Straw–lt.
311		3827	Golden Brown–pale
307		977	Golden Brown–lt.
4146		754	Peach–lt.
8		761	Salmon–lt.
9		760	Salmon
10		3712	Salmon–med.
893		224	Shell Pink–lt.
894	Z	223	Shell Pink–med.
896		3721	Shell Pink–dk.
167		597	Turquoise
1039		3810	Turquoise–dk.
214		368	Pistachio Green–lt.
215		320	Pistachio Green–med.
216		367	Pistachio Green–dk.
387		712	Cream
376	W w	842	Beige Brown–vy. lt.
378		841	Beige Brown–lt.
8581		647	Beaver Gray–med.
905	R	646	Beaver Gray–dk.
401		844	Beaver Gray–ultra dk.

Step 2: Backstitch (1 strand)

896		3721	Shell Pink–dk.
403		310	Black

Step 3: French Knot (1 strand)

403	•	310	Black

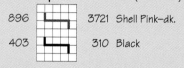

Gingham Santa

Stitch Count:	Fabrics	Finished Size
48 x 103	Aida 11	4⅜" x 9⅜"
	Aida 14	3⅜" x 7⅜"
	Aida 18	2⅝" x 5¾"
	Hardanger 22	2⅛" x 4⅝"

Top

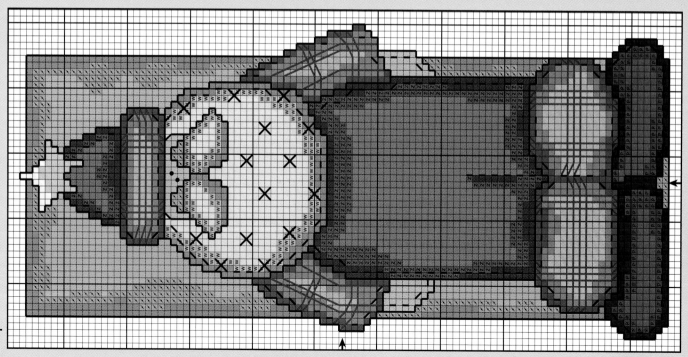

Anchor   DMC

Step 1: Cross Stitch (2 strands)

Anchor		DMC	
386		746	Off White
886		677	Old Gold–vy. lt.
891		676	Old Gold–lt.
271		3713	Salmon–vy. lt.
11		351	Coral
25		3326	Rose–lt.
27		899	Rose–med.
59		326	Rose–vy. dk.
154		3755	Baby Blue
213		369	Pistachio Green–vy. lt.
214		368	Pistachio Green–lt.
216		367	Pistachio Green–dk.
363		436	Tan
370		434	Brown–lt.

Step 2: Backstitch (1 strand)

59		326	Rose–vy. dk.
147		312	Navy Blue–lt.
216		367	Pistachio Green–dk.
403		310	Black

Step 3: French Knot (1 strand)

978		3223	Navy Blue–vy. lt.
216		367	Pistachio Green–dk.

Holiday Floral

Stitch Count: 79 x 34

Fabrics	Finished Size
Aida 11	7⅛" x 3⅛"
Aida 14	5⅝" x 2⅜"
Aida 18	4⅜" x 1⅞"
Hardanger 22	3⅝" x 1½"

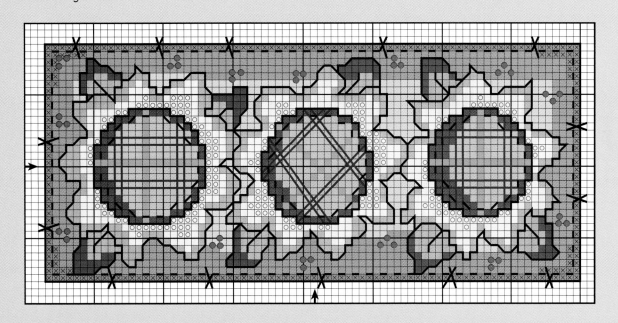

Three Stars

Stitch Count: 20 x 52

Fabrics	Finished Size
Aida 11	1⅞" x 4¾"
Aida 14	1⅜" x 3¾"
Aida 18	1⅛" x 2⅞"
Hardanger 22	⅞" x 2⅜"

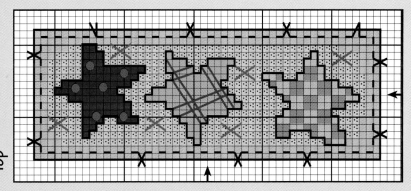

Winter Wear

Stitch Count: 42 x 49

Fabrics	Finished Size
Aida 11	3⅞" x 4½"
Aida 14	3" x 3½"
Aida 18	2⅜" x 2¾"
Hardanger 22	1⅞" x 2¼"

Plaid Pine

Stitch Count: 38 x 55

Fabrics	Finished Size
Aida 11	3½" x 5"
Aida 14	2¾" x 3⅞"
Aida 18	2⅛" x 3"
Hardanger 22	1¾" x 2½"

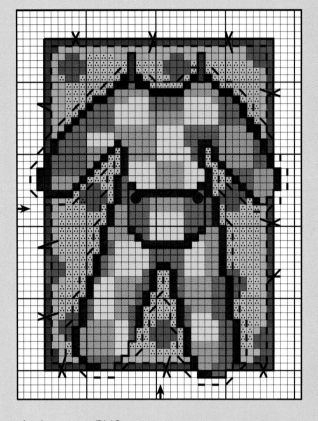

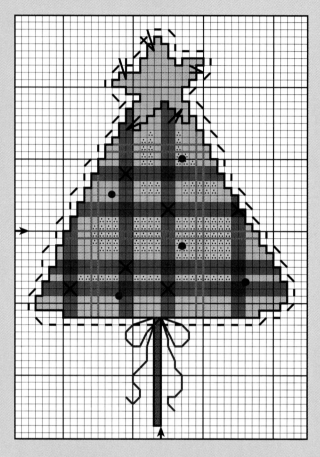

Anchor   DMC

Step 1: Cross Stitch (2 strands)

891		676	Old Gold–lt.
271		3713	Salmon–vy. lt.
25		3326	Rose–lt.
42		335	Rose
59		326	Rose–vy. dk.
978		322	Navy Blue–vy. lt.
213		369	Pistachio Green–vy. lt.
214		368	Pistachio Green–lt.
216		367	Pistachio Green–dk.
879		890	Pistachio Green–ultra dk.
370		434	Brown–lt.

Step 2: Backstitch (1 strand)

42		335	Rose
59		326	Rose–vy. dk.
403		310	Black

Step 3: Baby Buttons

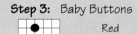   Red

Step 4: Beads

 62032 Frosted Cranberry

For The Birds

Stitch Count: 65 x 80

Fabrics / Finished Size

Fabrics	Finished Size
Aida 11	5⅞" x 7¼"
Aida 14	4⅝" x 5¾"
Aida 18	3⅝" x 4½"
Hardanger 22	3" x 3⅝"

Anchor	DMC

Step 1: Cross Stitch (2 strands)

Anchor			DMC	
386			746	Off White
886			677	Old Gold–vy. lt.
891			676	Old Gold–lt.
328			3341	Apricot
11			351	Coral
9			760	Salmon
25			3326	Rose–lt.
27			899	Rose–med.
42			335	Rose
59			326	Rose–vy. dk.
154			3755	Baby Blue (1 strand)
154			3755	Baby Blue
978			322	Navy Blue–vy. lt. (1 strand)
978			322	Navy Blue–vy. lt.
147			312	Navy Blue–lt. (1 strand)
147			312	Navy Blue–lt.
213			369	Pistachio Green–vy. lt.
214			368	Pistachio Green–lt. (1 strand)
214			368	Pistachio Green–lt.
216			367	Pistachio Green–dk. (1 strand)
216			367	Pistachio Green–dk.
942			738	Tan–vy. lt.
363			436	Tan
370			434	Brown–lt.
397			453	Shell Gray–lt.
398			452	Shell Gray–med.

399			451	Shell Gray–dk.

Step 2: Backstitch (1 strand)

59		326	Rose–vy. dk.
216		367	Pistachio Green–dk.
403		310	Black

Step 3: Long Stitch (1 strand)

403		310	Black

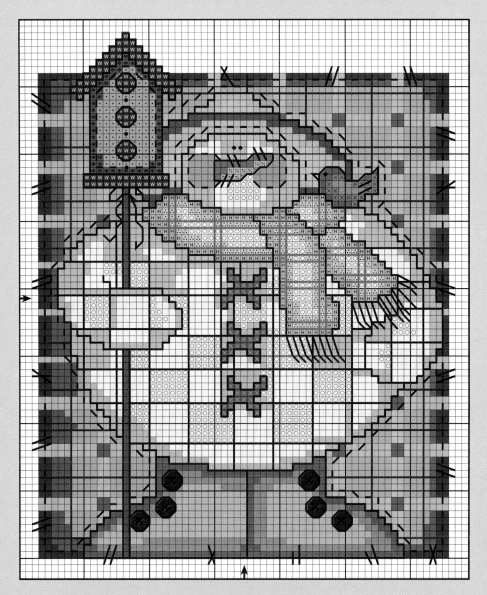

Metric Equivalency Chart

mm-millimetres   cm-centimetres
inches to millimetres and centimetres

inches	mm	cm	inches	cm	inches	cm
1/8	3	0.3	9	22.9	30	76.2
1/4	6	0.6	10	25.4	31	78.7
1/2	13	1.3	12	30.5	33	83.8
5/8	16	1.6	13	33.0	34	86.4
3/4	19	1.9	14	35.6	35	88.9
7/8	22	2.2	15	38.1	36	91.4
1	25	2.5	16	40.6	37	94.0
1 1/4	32	3.2	17	43.2	38	96.5
1 1/2	38	3.8	18	45.7	39	99.1
1 3/4	44	4.4	19	48.3	40	101.6
2	51	5.1	20	50.8	41	104.1
2 1/2	64	6.4	21	53.3	42	106.7
3	76	7.6	22	55.9	43	109.2
3 1/2	89	8.9	23	58.4	44	111.8
4	102	10.2	24	61.0	45	114.3
4 1/2	114	11.4	25	63.5	46	116.8
5	127	12.7	26	66.0	47	119.4
6	152	15.2	27	68.6	48	121.9
7	178	17.8	28	71.1	49	124.5
8	203	20.3	29	73.7	50	127.0

Index